June
July 29 7-800 pm
2020

attendance

rocio carlos and rachel mcleod kaminer

the operating system print//document

ATTENDANCE

ISBN: 978-1-946031-32-7
Library of Congress Control Number: 2018948545
copyright © 2018 by Rocío Carlos and Rachel McLeod Kaminer
edited and designed by ELÆ [Lynne DeSilva-Johnson]

This text was set in ALincolnFont, Europa, Gill Sans, Minion, Franchise, and OCR-A Standard.

Books from The Operating System are distributed to the trade by SPD/Small Press Distribution, with ePub and POD via Ingram, with production by Spencer Printing, in Honesdale, PA, in the USA.

2018-19 OS System Operators
CREATIVE DIRECTOR/FOUNDER/MANAGING EDITOR: ELÆ [Lynne DeSilva-Johnson]
DEPUTY EDITOR: Peter Milne Greiner
CONTRIBUTING EDITORS: Kenning JP Garcia, Adrian Silbernagel
JOURNEYHUMAN / SYSTEMS APPRENTICE: Anna Winham
SOCIAL SYSTEMS / HEALING TECH: Curtis Emery
VOLUNTEERS and/or ADVISORS: Adra Raine, Alexis Quinlan, Clarinda McLow, Bill Considine, Careen Shannon, Joanna C. Valente, Michael Flatt, L. Ann Wheeler, Jacq Greyja

The operating system is a member of the Radical Open Access Collective, a community of scholar-led, not-for-profit presses, journals and other open access projects. Now consisting of 40 members, we promote a progressive vision for open publishing in the humanities and social sciences.

Learn more at: http://radicaloa.disruptivemedia.org.uk/about/

Your donation makes our publications, platform and programs possible! We <3 You.
bit.ly/growtheoperatingsystem

the operating system
141 Spencer Street #203
Brooklyn, NY 11205
www.theoperatingsystem.org
operator@theoperatingsystem.org

attendance

for Theandrew Jerrod Clayborn
for the flora and the fauna
in this year of drought and fires

(A documentary work of attending to the year. The term was born from Rocío's description of going outside every morning to check on every thing that grows in her backyard. Together we decided one of us would attend to the flora and one of us would attend to the fauna. Of course, we found it difficult to stay in our own lanes. The whole world crept in: Family, friends and community; politics, atrocity, tragedy; literally the world. The book is presented in the notes and poems of both poets, beginning with a month in the voice of Rachel alternating with the same month in the voice of Rocío.)

Later we talked about it. Neither of us remembers exactly what conversations happened before we made our plan. But I met Rocío in the bar on Spring Street to make notes with her pen on a paper napkin. We'll start Attendance in January. On solstice I'm in North Carolina making the fire in the backyard with Amber; that is where the year begins. In Los Ángeles the year begins again with a long night and something that will turn into bruises. And again when Zoë goes out to Joshua Tree with me. We set up camp in a backcountry site. She's freezing and we laugh a lot and talk about dark complicated families and healing. We drive back. The next day her dad dies, and so it is that Zoë begins two thousand sixteen before any of us. The 6th, the Feast of Epiphany, is the other first day of the year. There are no epiphanies but there is rain.

—

[1 January] coyote crossing the road. Or enormous hindquarters of a jackrabbit

[2] the bird that takes an interest in us. the unseen inhabitants of root system tunnels, their camouflaged smooth holes. the raven, the noise of its wings in flight

woke up and wrote *Just try to want different things*. Sleeping cold in the desert—UNDER THE SKY—a long night. The moon rose. Then only rose another inch. Then only like two inches more, holding water the whole time. After the limited pink light of dawn, yellow and cream wash out the colors again. But having seen the red gold and green and purple, they stay and keep glowing from underneath

[4] the loud birds in the bamboo thicket in the courtyard and the sense of the blocks down Seventh, beauty of their trees and shade

when I dream the dreams take a turn

[5] corvids puffed up, giant, ruffling their wing feathers, breast feathers, tail feathers. And the two hawks circling their pines on the hill above Rocío's, she hears their call

[6] hawk, hummingbird. The hawk on a light pole over the Arroyo Parkway; the hummingbird on a wire tiny and in a small soft rain

[7] Rocío and I exit her house, after plant attendance and after Lady stretches out on me. On the wires strung along the telephone poles on Raber Street, two mourning doves. Each to their own section. The sky is glory, again. Rain and cold making it possible

[8] the Huntington without a camera. Hummingbirds, then driving home, sky lowering, pigeons or doves in flocks

[9] parrots in the persimmon trees, Alice's backyard. No leaves left, only ten green San Gabriel parrots

[10] small dogs, one cared for, one lost on a street corner and looking frantic or mad. Quiet Sunday birds on the light poles in Boyle Heights, and walking across the Fourth Street bridge, a fast bird shape flying straight down. Water in the river channel

[11] the pigeons rising up past the edge of the freeway. Where the Arroyo Seco drains into the river channel. But also, sitting that in-between place on the edge of Elysian Park, hearing birds; going to see them, but only hearing them for the first half hour. The ravines are so steep that there are birds in trees above me, across from me, below me. Eventually I get to see them and in color

[12] two dozen parrots roosted together on telephone wire—or light signal wire? at the fork in Pasadena. Up the way, flying parrots look ill at ease in flight out in the open by the watershed. Nine crows fly east, playful dives and proximity adjustments, nipping at each other's heels like a pack of wolves. Sun up, the sky cleared of all the gorgeous stratus from last night. Just the haze catching the changing light that warms from cool to purple, pink-orange, and then warm pale blue

[13] Really strange, really specific dreams. Fuck. I don't want to write any of it down

pigeons in a flock again, the same flock? rising over the same confluence. My inept description for what they do, the shifting matrix pulling their flight vectors in unknown directions. Sine curves? Three dimensions + a fourth? The color of the sky, and texture, feel as important (as emblematic, as appearing) as the birds and animals do. And the light this morning hit the front range of the San Gabriels so I could finally read how it's oriented redacted. The west section catches almost full flight at sun up (it was glowing pinkorangeochre then *yellow*) and I guess it runs west-southwest to east-northeast. So there's a break, a point of meeting at an angle, just above the Hahamongna watershed draining the front range. And oh that's also the pass up above it, the 2, Angeles Crest. The Arroyo Seco: A watershed of 46.7 square miles. Part of the Eulalia tract in 1834?

[14] lost in a song from Have One On Me until I'm halfway up the arroyo, so I don't see if the pigeons are rising from the channel confluence when I drive by. When I wake up to it, a few pigeons, then up ahead I see the hawk coming. Still; facing south on one of the light poles. I turn my head as I steer the car into a right-hand curve—always in the left lane, always snug to the concrete divider—I swear as I pass below the bird turns too, body poised and dark except for light feathers at the scruff of the neck and breast, but head and gaze following my head craning over my left shoulder, cold pressed to the window. Immediately I have to adjust the steering. The mountains and colors are next. The sun may be up but hasn't broken through the clouds. A cool glow in the rest of the sky and clouds. The front range is massive this morning. They're pastel, matte pastel, blue purple. Gray under blue under faint pinking violet and ochre. How do I take attendance without the sky and terrain—where, or where else, can I show up?

C.D. Wright died on Tuesday. She was 67, Arkansas born, wasn't she. Jen posts, "And It Came To Pass," and I send it to T unconsciously. She was born on January 6th, Feast of Epiphany, 1949.

[15] hawks, but not, so, vultures, circling over the steep hill where Forest Lawn borders Griffith Park. Deer I don't see. Then driving back across the 134, such a fat hawk, facing east. We both see it, Zoë saying how she always sees them and no one else sees them with her

[16] people's small dogs

[17] mourning doves hooting above my building's inner courtyard, echoing and from above. Joanna Newsom singing a while later, about them howling

[18] on the way back from the grocery store, a wren or sparrow. The little ones that hop and bob their heads around to peer at you, with different layered browns on their wings. It was pecking at

something on the sidewalk on Eighth and waited to dart out of the way until I was almost upon it. It didn't fly, or even ruffle its feathers or shake them out, just ducked under the tarped fence by a construction site

[19] on the way across the conjunction, no flocking pigeons but instead a lined-up squadron, all on the concrete rail with imitation balustrades

Then a scrub jay, a hummingbird in flight, and a ruffled raven/crow after the rain began, on one of the poles over an accident on the 110 south. Finally—FINALLY—I was so anxious for it or for *something anything*— Hawk. In a treetop rather than a light pole. Keeping its own counsel. Faced to the west. Their bird bodies seem big in the most perfect way to me

[20] the same cloud of pigeons over the aqueducts. Realized I drive by there (almost without exception) two minutes before "sunrise." First light before I wake up now and that's how I know solstice has passed, the cool light that just barely glows

On the way down the arroyo I want to see a hawk and so I look up and past the light poles, to the sycamores east of me. There is one, perched in the gold green leaves left on the top branches. *OR,* on the way down the arroyo my peripheral vision notices the desired shape and swivels my head before it's passed—explain how else my glance lands exactly on the still bird and nowhere else. *OR,* I wish to see, and do

[21] Scout, sphinx on the guard rails of the front porch at Raber Street. Hummingbirds at sunset playing chase. So I be with Rocío at home and then meet Jaquita at Sonny's. It's good.

[22] see almost no one, driving the usual up the arroyo, but 20 minutes earlier than normal. So the sky pastels are brilliant and come in broad stripes, swathes, but sunrise happens right as I arrive at the alta dena; the high plateau that lays out just before the face and canyons of the San Gabriel front range. Y que más. Parrots. Pigeons. A squirrel

the warm animal of your body Noticing I notice women, their bodies and my own, differently than other bodies

[redacted]

[23] parrots in a flock where I don't expect them, over on Washington at Arlington, but, now I know their frantic sound and shape in open air.

[24] did I see? did I look

[25] the flock of pigeons *was* wheeling and in a kind of ascending and descending figure 8 at angles, as when a coin was spinning and is close to stopping flat. The parrots, did I realize how *many* there are? And how widely distributed? I just thought of them as "the Pasadena parrots." Also they totally flap. There's no other way to describe the feeling they give me of flailing.

[26] a couple crows crisscrossing campus, and *then*, near 3 p.m., down the arroyo, thought I saw another one across the freeway on a light pole, because of its relative height. But NO. It was a hawk *Leaning*, body shifted forward feet still gripping, and what? Adjusting? About to dive for it, prey or flight? Distracted and fixated? In any case there it was facing downstream and distinctly gorgeous.

Which reminds me, hawks. What redtail ones do that's different than some other's habits. They sit. Watch and wait. Choose their time to move. It's like the fucking ruby-throated hummingbirds all over again, making their shape an icon, feeling it slide into place with a solid CLACK. A sound like that but an och sound

[27] south on the Arroyo: A hawk shape turning out to be a crow standing up tall, almost leaning back. That was in the afternoon. In the morning, colors: grey yellows, winter sky with silhouettes—not all stick figure trees—palms of both kinds, bare sycamores, pines. Cell towers too. Then, glowing sherbet colors: pinks, golds. Making the other side of the sky glow too. Later I see the dusty brown yellow encircling the basin, visible on the open horizons, and it clicks: Why there was enough material to light up in colors on such a clear day with clouds already dissipated by the time the sun was an inch up the horizon. Then candy pink and candy blue

[28] daybreak at 5:26, the almanac said, so that was my alarm. When I went out to my car at six it was barely first light. I didn't realize there was such a length in between. So far, the crow caw, the skunk smell, the crow shape poking at itself, dried horse manure, hen squawk, bird call I don't know, parrot flap.

To write about myself as a creature, or someone I regard with desire and attraction—that's one thing. It's different (is it?) those other regards. No? Yet to see people as people is...

[29] dark up to work. Birdsong there, another new one. The human adolescents I work with all day, funny and sweet and original and aggressive and needy and just, if I'm a creature they are creatures too, in a way that is comforting. Last night Rocío and I had drinks and she told me about the amazing creature who hunts as an orchid

On Orange Grove, headed for the intersection back to the Arroyo, I drive under a hummingbird. It's stopped / hovering in place so as to appear still, exactly over my lane up at the height of the trees and palms. I see it ahead of me and can't believe it hasn't moved by the time I drive underneath. Mistletoe, I think. It was hung there for me. Or someone else? Or it was holding up for us invisible mistletoe. Stopped in flight

[30] a seagull, the ones with white head feathers and grey on their wings, on top of an SRO on the northeast side of Seventh Street between Kohler and San Pedro.

[31] no creatures so far. It's raining, not even many dogs out for walk. Reading *H is for Hawk*

On the drive back from King Taco with Eva, a crow, on a light pole, before the Seventh Street bridge

in between, more in between than usual

> dark
> barely first light
> not dark but not sunrise
> past daybreak
> before sun up
> the sun an inch up the horizon
>
> transverse range

corvids

the raven, the noise of its wings in flight
puffed up, giant, ruffling their wing feathers, breast, tail, cheek feathers

nine crows fly east, play dives and proximity adjustments,
nipping each other's heels like a pack of wolves

shape turning out to be a crow standing up tall, leaning back
crow caw, crow shape poking at itself, crow,
crow late morning flying east overhead

raven, long pinion missing from their wing
gap   seen rather than heard

hummingbird

on a wire tiny and in a small soft rain

towards the arroyo
hover in place
appear still at the height
of the trees and palms

holding up for us

another month of them
none in color

paloma

pigeons rising up past the edge of the freeway where the Arroyo Seco drains
into the river channel

pigeons in a flock again, the same flock rising over the same confluence
shifting matrix pulling their flight vectors in unknown directions
sine curves in three dimensions

I don't see if the pigeons are rising from the channel confluences

on the way across the conjunction,
no flocking pigeons but instead a lined-up squadron,
all on the concrete rail with imitation balustrades

the same cloud of pigeons over the aqueducts;
realize I pass by almost without exception two minutes before sunrise

flock of pigeons wheeling and in a kind of ascending and descending
figure 8 at angles,
as when a coin is spinning and is close to stopping flat

that pigeon flock lined up on the same concrete bridge over the arroyo
and river channels,
ten minutes before sun up when they take flight and bustle and wheel

not dark but not sunrise, more in between than usual,
and the pigeons aren't there on the balustrade
nor wheeling in their weird flight

mammal

see in the dark
crossroad
frantic or mad

deer I don't see
soft warm animal of your body
noticing I notice bodies, and my own, newly
Redacted.
When hard soften

seeing is looking except on a road
skunk smell

regard me as a creature
attract
differ,
those other regards. No?
to see people as people yet—

if I'm a creature they are too,
in a way that is comforting

no creatures so far, it's raining

Sky lowering, sky cleared

color and texture
as important, as emblematic,
as appearing,
as the birds and animals

mountains and colors
matte pastel, blue purple,
gray under blue under faint pinking violet and ochre

sky pastels are brilliant and come in broad stripes,
swathes, sunrise happens
the high plateau lays out before the face and canyons
San Gabriel front range

another side of the sky, cool light,
high plateau laid out before the face and canyons

in the morning, colors:
grey yellows
winter sky with silhouettes
then, glowing sherbet colors: pinks, golds
making the other side of the sky glow too

later, dusty brown yellow encircling the basin
enough material to light up in colors
on such a clear day at dawn

[January 6th- epiphany]

It rained all day

I took the meow blanket to the porch. I sat facing out toward the street. The rain was like bars, cool and wet, a cage of water. I was happy, alone and early in the day. I propped up my feet and let my coffee get cold.

I think the tree across the street is a piocha, or a paraíso. The city workers cut the canopy flat to avoid the power lines. Now it mimics the willow, the low branches hang down like embarrassed arms.

The gutter is a bed of yellow leaves.

Nikki came with his top coat wet.
The mint in the tiled pot is drowning
The rain is horizontal, or L-shaped. It points like angry stingers.
Scout is angry at the rain, she thinks I did it, she shouts at me.

Later, I do a lap, yes, yes everything is watered, the lavender looses its wild oils; I wish I had a pine to marry the lavender to.

[January 7th- the seventh day]

No rest for the dirt. Even when it's laying there, it's working. The pumpkin in the compost is melting back into the earth. Everything is silver with water. The clover gloat over the dead winter grass. See us, the clover slurs, see our long lemon stalks, our trumpet flower. The clover is a jerk.

Early the hawks screeched then the three circled in thanks.

Sunny but fucking cold.

And then we walked to Sonny's.

[January 8- Friday]

I followed Scout out. She waddled determined, she always brushes under the Rosemary.

Rosemary= sea spray. Rocío Marino.

The colibrís swing high then low, ululating. They are waiting for a bloom.

To DO:
Plant amapolas.

And then, the new year blurs

      Somewhere a boy throws a fit, the snows come.
      The snow pack fortifies itself.

The hillside is green, even as the trees are bare.
The arroyo is full of dirty water but I am so glad.

P-22 is cured of mange.
I wonder if the deer eat ice plant.

The bougainvillea pays court to the porch
I plant California poppies
The amapolas that make Ana giddy with laughter
sweet peas for height, little circus banners
nasturtium to ramble in orange and yellow
lobelias for purple
And three lavenders for the smell (I want to die eaten by) such a plant/

The cleaning, and clearing. The leaves, all the tiny veins
I turn soil, some of the compost isn't finished; I don't care. The avocado skins are stubborn little shits.
Poppies, ivy, plumeria.
I built an arch for the garden gate.
The jasmine is coming. The morning glory is a greedy vine.
The magnolia drops old branches big as antlers.
The mocking bird won't have Dizzy to kick around this year.
Oh stay scrub jay don't go, the aloe salutes us, little salmon-colored parasols. Here come colibrís again. Huitzil. Colibrí, throat bright as a wound. Trill trill trill.

I see you.

Day One

I confused my memory of last New Year's Eve
with last Halloween
one rained and the other bit with cold
we drank and shouted in the crowds of people
or we drank and laughed while Disney movies
played in the background
strangers in costumes smiled at us
or your relatives talk amongst themselves
a selfie in my silver party dress in the bathroom of a home in San Bernardino
or cupcakes and prayers of thanks for a roof, an oven.
We stay because it is too cold to leave
or we passed the shrieking sirens, the red lights on the wet world.
Which part is true, which part is regret
what day is it, how old are we now
at four in the morning, yes
the mother of the girl next door crying in the street
So He Just Kills You? So You Just Get Killed?
The veil over downtown, the Pasadena mountains full of sleeping coyotes
somewhere the ocean heaves onto rock, somewhere the year turns in on itself
translation is like those days before the first day of something
when you get out of bed to see what is preserved and what is not there.

Rain

Rain in the morning, L-shaped stingers of water.

(that stray gray comes with his top coat wet)

We look out at the street; glory comes tomorrow/
we leave shoes out for the last gift of January:
the hummingbird on the telephone wire as the rain softens,
early for the bloom/

the world has not ended/so we walk:

(*attendance* is counting and greeting)

eyeing the barren spot where
nasturtium will go, or the bright poppies in March.
The crow, the red-capped woodpecker drilling into the telephone pole
the calico's determined waddle under the rosemary bush;
she brushes the smell of church all over my legs, expectant.
The lavender looses its wild oils,
a pine somewhere proposes marriage.

Epiphanies are for the free and we, my dear, are not.

Paraíso

From here, the paradise mimics the willow
low branches hang down like embarrassed arms.
Between the paradise and you: no man's land/
pregnancy/ a purgatory/ an eden/ graves,
grey clouds/ muted sounds/ echoes/ sighs and murmurs
the flames here and there on a dry landscape/
the fine down of a body that suffers cold
the harvest of hearts/ a line in the dirt/ the door.

You wish for a wall to keep you away but
(the thing about a wall is): who is going to pay for it?

The Seventh Day

No ides come in January
so we are spared the middles of things
we grit our teeth as ambulances pass
and wake up at the end of the month
buds push up from soil even as famous people begin dying.
Everything is silver with water
the gutter a bed of yellow leaves
the arroyo brown with runoff
a scrub jay shakes and sings in the stone bowl
we are relieved when there are no phone calls,
when the jasmine keeps climbing
but we understand
January has come but not gone.

[1 February] crow

[2] loud birds in the bamboo, past daybreak. That pigeon flock lined up on the same concrete bridge over the arroyo and river channels, ten minutes before sun up when they take flight and bustle and wheel

[3] not dark but not sunrise, in between / more in between than usual, and the pigeons aren't there lined up on the balustrade nor wheeling in their weird flight

[4] a crow, late morning, flying east overhead. One of its (their?) long pinions is missing from its (their?) wing—I see it rather than hear it—the gap in the left wing makes a startling contrast

[5] No pigeons on the balustrade for me. And the bamboo birds aren't as loud either

[6] Pigeon, at the Los Feliz exit off the 5, by the discarded "homeless and hungry, please help" sign which has a spider web drawn on it. Hummingbird at the feeder on the 11th floor of Los Feliz Towers

[7] The kind of sparrow/hatch with tail feathers that fan a bit, loop de loops by the roof pool's railing. Cheep! Cheep! ...cheep! Later, parrots. (Amazonas, Rocío calls them for me.) I didn't think they were down here in this neighborhood. Five head east, one splits off to the south

[8] Over each road at intervals, three crows, all flapping. One bird—swallow?—banking and gliding in a curve to the left. Also the red rust pigeon in my paint varnished courtyard made from an alley. Standing near the stairs. Both legs banded, tracking devices? one red and one blue.

[9] Crows going west and over the road. More than three.
The little birds and big ones who kind of skid/brace their wings to shift shoulders up and feet down, landing or swooping in a fly by. Immediate and precise.
Rebecca texts me that now love does not exist or when it does it lasts like four days and then ghosts. Love *ghosts*.

I think of my not twin not sister and our mirroring and matching and parallel play; the synced swimming that was all freestyle and long limbs full length, pulling water, propulsion, holding the rotation and the glide. Glances to calibrate with her. To see us.
(being an animal, feeling that other people are creatures, it helps. It helps what?)

ASH WEDNESDAY

pigeons roosting or nesting in Hollywood on Sunset, with young new ones.
the wolf dog we see on Colorado in Eagle Rock
the small child in her parent's arms, delighted to see ashes on their forehead which match her own mark
the other children, their half squall half wail kind of crying at the back of the cathedral

[11] Spending an afternoon with Monice, then Ana and Rocío sobremesa, the book art, connecting to Ana's tearfulness and deep things. Walking our walk down to Sonny's, laughter, even. One glass of wine. The walk back.

[12] I stay indoors except to talk to Mom out in the courtyard hallway and get better phone reception.

I watch the strip of blue I can see out the window between the beams—from the lifeboat while I read. On and off throughout the day there are the coo hoots of a mourning dove. It makes me know how much cooler it must be in the courtyard than up on the open air roof. When it's dark I go out for one glass of wine and see the mural on the corner of Seventh and Mill has been painted over. *H is for Hawk* before bed. I feel (not for the first time again) how naked it is to write about animals, both Helen MacDonald and T. H. White...

[13] missed most of the day

[14] I shut myself in again, reading, hearing the courtyard mourning dove, and thinking about *H is for Hawk*'s wildness

[15] Greyhounds on walks. Rocío writes about the coyote (its nothing behind its eyes in that moment) and wishes for them a nice meal not made of kitties

[16] Full sun on the drive—pigeons on the balustrade—they all face east except the ones not sitting still.
On my way out of work a creature watching me half visible over a wall. I make a move to see and it pulls back over and down. Lizard? Cat? Chipmunk? Squirrel? Bird?

Driving home, avoided much outdoor time today. Am I living wrong? "Just not living right"—I used to see so many—be among so many—animals all day that I could distinguish the visitors. (My visitors as compared to neighbors. Appearances and visits.) Now I can't, they all seem to be visiting as their sign and seal. Not every creature is a visitor! Or in the city every animal is a Damascus road, every single one?

Two crows in the top of a pine
The pigeons lined up sun basking
birdsong all day long, birds I don't know

[17] dry half the day. It rained the second half. I had tea with Brande on the outside courtyard-porch of the cafe. The walls of plants there

[18] and rained hard in the night and in the morning I put on my usual black shoes, stepped outside to check, then took them 100% off and put on hiking boots. Happy for that all day. Three crows flying east, at intervals along my route, in rain. Saw Zoë, saw Rocío—visiting the cats. Hear, with Ana and Rocío, the most amazing bird recently

[19] Looking for hawk, light poles—there. One tall sycamore that shares the arroyo road channel. Facing north, is that human of me? I think, I think... Need to attend to the topography—surveying a scene up and or a prey and or napping? Later coming down the 2 there are two doing a spiral—banking on the air currents eddying in watershed of Glendale between Verdugo and

Yes. No railing There
Now—helicopter; falling sleep here
It's the morning—or was

[20] redtail over Lida with Rocío around twelve. High sun—unusual birdsong in the bamboo and on Divers. Later with Chiwan, driving east on the 60 to try and make San Bernardino before dark thirty. Past Diamond Bar, a pole strung the freeway with a hawk tensed to hunt the dusk prey in the roadside clear cut meadow

[21] pigeons I see and hear on our downtown walk make me think more about pigeons. Dismissed; not seen as wild. I will look up their natural history

[22] and there are two big corvids—ravens? a yard apart on a telephone wire. They are fluffing themselves in the heat, it lets the breeze into their underwings. The crows at work have been building a nest in one of the six tall palms over my school building. One of the crows likes long, noticeable sticks or stalks, but flies a path designed to throw (who?) off the track. It's dodging and weaving. But the palm is a high exposed place and the location of the nest is obvious. A crow came last spring came and dashed one of the nests over to eat the hummingbird eggs. Later when I walk to and from a night event, I'm happy about the temperature of the night, the quiet on Eighth, the people walking and awake. On the way home I'm writing and I see again how the human bodies are going to be what I write about too. The sign—BELIEVE IN PSYCHIC VISIONS—a palm of a hand on the wall, a large sign. And the answer to the questions as a list:

> smoke, both kinds
> gin in vapors of body heat metabolized as much by skin as liver
> lavender
> lime
> iron in the mouth
> chlorine
> ~~ocean~~ salt
> ~~bulimia~~ acid
> oats or grits
> vitamin C; cranberry from the capsules that burst in your mouth between your molars
> a week in the forest
> poplar and steel
> willow, sycamore, clay
> ash after it's lost the flavor of its wood
> charred wood still distinguishable. white cedar. red cedar.
> pine, sap sticks to you after you come home and scrub
> it feels good, clean dirt in a texture
> camp soap; damp forest floor duff

[23] Our human species has obvious-to-all-of-us differentiation. We can read ourselves as individuals and tribal collectives, peoples. Do other animals? Humans aren't the most numerous species, but for a technological apex predator/pest infestation, there sure are a lot of us. Do bees, tuna, salmon, dragonflies, koalas, horses see themselves this way? What's the animal with a population numbering closest to seven or eight billion? Human, perception limits itself (here, now) to domesticated individuals

was I in attendance is that when I saw the bee

[24] Bookmaking with Rocío, her hands and the line of her hair; Ana's drawing for the back cover keeps looking like a hummingbird

[25] the wasp bees at Alice's.

I really wanted to kiss you. It felt like I could kiss you.

[26] Dead bird, warbler (I look it up for hours, grey, yellow, markings)
Songbird at the Huntington late afternoon, after a day devoted to human songwriting

[27] plants. Bees must be some nearby. And a small dog fierce at his reflection

[28] marine layer so the bridge balustrade has no sun salutation pigeons

[29] But all this time, the crows making their nests, or what, What are they building?

paloma

no pigeons on the balustrade
rust red pigeon in the courtyard made from an alley
full sun, pigeons on the balustrade, all face east except the ones not standing still
pigeons lined up sun basking
pigeons appearing downtown;
what word for this *appearing* that means *in the ear*?
more about pigeons, dismissed, not wild, a natural history
today, marine layer so the bridge balustrade has no sun salutation pigeons

redtails

looking for hawk, light poles—there.
one tall sycamore that shares arroyo road channel
attend to the topography—surveying a scene up and or a prey and or a napping
later there are two spiral-banking on the air currents eddying over the watershed
redtail around noon. high sun
past Diamond Bar, a pole strung the freeway with a hawk
tensed up to hunt the dusk prey in the roadside clear-cut meadow

bees and

when I saw the bee
and the wasp bees
I really wanted to kiss you.
It felt like I could kiss you.
Plants. Bees, must be some nearby.

mammal

my not twin and our mirroring, matching, parallel play
free and longing limbs at full lengths
pulling water, propulsion, holding rotation, glide
glances calibrate with her, glances of us
being as animal, feeling other people creatures,
help,

mammal

> her hands and the line of her hair
> making
> I really wanted to kiss you. It felt like I could kiss you.

mammal

that repeated question in two, one underneath maybe;
how their fingers which would be new or wouldn't
that eighth of an inch dermis dry steeped in nicotine, tobacco;
much it means to love a lover who also knows fresh skin—
rough, calloused or stained; freshly washed, thoroughly rinsed: much

that I want to be skin to skin fresh and on clean bedding
how gradually more messed up in sweat, slide, in heat, chills: much

that I don't have or won't write the words but I have felt restless and right
have smelled it on you,
have passed back and forth the layering through one another's skin

fingers though
in my mouth, in not-my mouth, which I want to be mine
belong harshly to me

the intimacy of bathing you under a shower
ritual preparation as an act that makes sex proximate
feeling of all my skin
awake and in a slurred wakefulness
physically spaced in and out of my body

mammal

having an animal scent myself and coming after yours like an animal,
that as an animal I did
would, slip fingers between myself and slide-scoop two of them to taste
more than wet, holding together in a viscosity pleases, spider webs in dew
noticing my mouthing changed the taste, I mean, how I ate
this other palate
kiwi. curry. seaweed.
I'm not soaked
slow thicker-than-water bubble

every hand full of fingers tonight
write animal ~~appearances~~
attending ~~attendance~~

not blackberry, (repeat, repeat.)
Black raspberry.
Wild blueberry on the top of the balds in late summer.
our sides of cherries
corn, a sharp part of taste, that blue corn
that green tomato

February

A sophomore, February comes in too brash fanfares made of water. The bay laurel trees dry up, they've been dying for three years now, even as the saplings spiral bravely out of the foliage. Every time I hear a helicopter I'm not afraid it's some fugitive, loose in the back yards of my neighborhood— I'm afraid it's the fire department checking for ready kindling.
I've stopped raking the leaves. They'll keep the moisture in the soil longer.
This is some fucked up clay soil here. The water just runs off of it or it sits on the surface till moss comes to live.

I eat the lettuce and kale I grow. I see pill bugs mating on the leaves, earwigs milling around the roots. Who knows what happens in that soil at night, or even under my nose, too small for me to see. The lettuce leaves spiral out of their origin. There is that word again, spiral. That is the direction of nature, splitting cells, clouds of flaming gas, ocean currents that come to kill us all, unfurling ferns.

The echeveria's bloated petals, waiting for the end. They drop off and die and then they release little red veins, probes. The rise up as on feet and look for soil.

The heat, the eggs on the rocks in Death Valley.

Rain, come. Virgins in caves, plumed beauties. The moon rises, angels sing: yes/no/let come the torrent.

This morning- the rain, the near death of one Scout B. Calico. Coyote: it didn't bob up and down like an animal with joints and foot falls. It glided, as if on tracks, it cut through the world like a shark in water. The Bougainvillea shudders with the night's rain when I run down the wooden steps.

February comes in showy, pink peach blossoms on bare branches.
Geraniums get tall like eager ears but they have never bloomed
Tiny ruby-throat perches— little feet curling around the branch.
Ese pobre nopal tiene plaga.

I clear the crab grass from the ice-plant so as to clarify something to the men hired by my landlady.

Little figs, little twin heads.
I'm going to trim this canopy, put a little table under it. The pile of wood against the fence.
A sound across the street- tree falling over, the sound of roots loosening their grip. The great crack of movement in the inflexible.
Oh. It was only a bamboo partition.

***

Little cove of green.
Aloe hydra.
Passion flower- how many varieties?
How many kinds of suffering are there?
Purple blossoms crumpled like wedding tissue.
The jasmine little unlit wicks. The smell is like a strong cab(ernet) deep and swirling like the smoke under Pilár Ternera's arms.

Echeveria, pinwheels at festivals, parasols twirling.
The little wicker lights are up, the nights are wonderful back here, this way.
Coco drinks from the bird bath, stretched out like a lemur.
That stupid hedge with the sticky blue flowers is taunting me.
Come on nasturtium. Come on, you can make it.
The amapolas are up, girls in red dresses turning cartwheels.
The bad neighbor's voice troubles the trees.
The good neighbor walks his grandchild in the plants.

bad harvest, bad harvest.

Again Lent

A sophomore, February comes
too brash fanfares made of water
in fire country the bay laurels dry up
the prayer for rain is a fish's mouth mouthing
de donde cae la nieve
de donde viene la tercera hermana
que aburridos los ojos azules and things like that
Lent is a square surrounded on all sides by sand
the mountain of burning shrubs,
the devil's wilderness
or rivers; Jordan for example.
In our mouths, strange legends

Eurydice en Carnaval (for Sandra Bland)

Beyond as in el mas allá
beyond as in beyond the
beyond as in yonder and be
the bluest yonder
how blue do you sing
how black and blue must you be
and how white that noose
ghosts come with coins in their mouths
fat tongues say their alphabets, their numbers
remember the seasons, the months of the year
sing them and remember:
July is hot as a blue flame
December white with ash.
She went beyond her body
we say Happy February.

Evangeline

History is full of errors, forests primeval
and dead messengers.
Evangeline in the ferns, the heroine alone
in a place called Monrovia.
The heroine, *sola*
alone is a song
sung into the window pane
on those rainy days in June.

Leap Day

On varieties of passion flower:
how many kinds of suffering
a country slipped away when you weren't looking
the peaches of immortality hang from long-bed trucks in front of you
In the yard every morning, attendance:
jasmine, citruses sneak their green on you.
quarreling sparrows, bully mockingbirds
the coyote that almost ate your familiar.
You can't document it fast enough
and then you listen to a song and it all turns to Macondo.
Imagine sad waltzes: a klezmer, a pianola
or was it the shouting of white men instead?
There is nothing sadder than
a three/fourths time.

[1 March] Crows hide their nest building is that me then
Crows show off their best building is that me then
Just look so shiny brilliant while they do it

Dear y'all I write from below the hill over Solano Canyon where the human figures form a loose circle, it's clear to me as I pass that they are holy women, witch women holding their hands up for the city

[2] Lemon blossoms really are heavy in the air, and how does their smell get in my car at sun-up, are they heavier because of needing the bees to find them?
I don't share the intimacy of
anymore

[3] Fountain near Vermont, a bee is interested in me. Above La Tuna Canyon—up at its height—birds at play. In East Hollywood or South Los Feliz, the lemon trees are blossoming heaviness too

[4] Another crow with a pinion missing gap, right wing, closer to the body. Why do I think of crows as men, male? Crow women

[5] Dawn, on the roof, very little sleep and less desire to do so. The birds in the bamboo get louder and it's harder to separate their calls

The preknowing is the knowing. Or this kind of writing, making the notes for the work seem like the prework/pretext and the do not let your right hand know *that* the other is doing—Then making the notes the work only a while later. The premonition approaches the limit of knowing instantaneously.*

*What's the word for contemporaneously that refers to the moment/instant you're currently in? Knowing right away, knowing as soon as you know. I knew as soon as I knew

On the roof thinking of my book, how angry I realized it was later. (Also of earlier when I realized oh it's a heartbreak book and later oh it's sadness and grief.) Now feeling more / beyond into a more opened up, hopeful? belief about—it's *possible* to unknow—a kind of undoing is happening—there is a slide back from knowing or a towards uncertainty built with these knowings.

What I really want is to make the long cut from the bottom of your spine to the nape of your neck, fold it open and immediately wrap myself in your skin but I need to be patient, need to wait and finish sewing in the zipper.

[6] Sunday, crowded humans all day, just invisible pigeons and our people needs

[7] Crows. Walk to the grocery store. Light candles.

[8] a juvenile raccoon dead in the middle of Windsor (from Arroyo to Altadena Drive on the edge of Hahamongna). I got out of my car to take a picture. I was overwhelmed by the color of the blood on its head and by the intensity and uniformity of the unclosed eyes. I began to feel really and truly emotional. I don't cry over animals but this

In the afternoon a redheaded woodpecker dead near the center of a street in La Crescenta. It looks ALMOST asleep but is stretched wrongly, one of its wings, and turned/twisted the neck, head totally sideways. Again I almost fell apart with tears. Its colors and feathers were just: beautiful. so. beautiful.

La Tuna Canyon! It was supposed to be just a stop at the trailhead, but turned quickly into a wondrous (if ill-considered means no H_2O, no person to call rangers, no charged phone battery, etc.,) two hours. Lizards lizards lizards. A not-squirrel not-otter with shiny pelt and a stillness. Someone's husky dog on a good walk. And crows, so many crows. Playful with and against the wind gusts. "As the crow flies"—this idea, these directions, the travel over topography direct through. But crows play dip dive chase. And soar. More than my redtail does. My redtail is me sitting very very still and maybe sizing the scene over and over. I'm—am I less hawk, that hawk, and more crow? Want to be on the wind these days. Not on the branch.

[9] The redheaded woodpecker on the second day.

[10] Big fat redtail sitting glory on the pole, head in profile: hawkhead profile: a word better than beak is. And the redheaded woodpecker on the third day.

[12] Y'all that feelings are a firm of masochism
Like
Really know on tumblr tags
All feelings in the spectrum
But angry

Also that sex isn't feelings

[20] and then I didn't write for a week, write anything down
All I saw were birds that meant anything to me
After what I told you, told Rocío, I knew there was being a problem
No mammals modeling for me a way to be, live
Birds which cover their skin in well-spiked feathers, camouflaged spines
and fly away from their nests as a distraction from their places
Badly hidden technique, which isn't to say ineffective
Hawks, more than once, and in the places that have meant things to me
Crows at all times, and or ravens, I still don't learn the difference except close up
Mourning doves, one and two at a time, my favorite current metaphor epiphany emblem for of my future, even in the slatted courtyard light, their call echoing literally, their days too.

[Redacted]

The other things that was a sneaking-in-and-out suspicion is also confirm. Trying to figure (paloma!) out what the feelings *mean* when there are all the feelings, that doesn't really help navigate (safely or not) amongst the waves of them and their water/liquid turbulence. I mean duh. Right? But it dawns on me like rocket science (but no really, like a really intuitive path through a calculus _____ what's that word name again, the step-by-step slowed in its motion by your sensing-ahead brain, giving you time to feel it unfolding, falling apart loose and open in your gentle hands), rocket science, that I amnesia and amnesia again until there's a sticking point of the repetition and a might-as-well choice (feels so little bitty these choices the ones I can actually move on) to write something down.

At all times a heartsick feeling of distance from Amy's daily life rhythms. Heartbeat I can't match up with from far away, but there's the feeling and then there's the fulfilling it. The otters in another river, me in this other one, toxic but is it toxic to me?

At all times reading. For more than twelve hours at a stretch, barely rotated positions (lying down front, back, side; sitting) and locations (this bed, that bed, chair at the table). It makes a hyperreal vision when and if there is an outdoor moment—gopher hole head/second

Other than Alice's body, and mine, there are the not crows. The birds. And my own, mine when in isolation.

[Second Day of Spring]—Your brain is all over your body

Pigeon-paloma (that talk with Alice) flew at me—no through where I was—fanned out back feathers and wings, feather fan brushing me down my face, from the top/crown of my head (or the second chakra the eye one) down across my face, the skin of my face.

Hello (Ana was there, it's all I said, stopped but didn't startle, which is strange now I think of it, I always do even when I ~~see~~ watch it coming) *hello, messenger. What's your message?* What are you telling me? Baptism, the sprinkling kind. Or the Jordan River holy ghost kind

[23] I didn't know what I was looking at
I *like* being alone in the middle of the night reading
I liked being awake with you next to me sleeping, too
Sometimes

I have no impulse control when it comes to books—Just that one bit more—Just a little further—Zero

[28] In March everything goes to shit. to blood, or no like, bad humors. There are still some sightings: another hummingbird on a wire directly overhead; another fat fat hawk sitting still over sycamore groves; a hawk playing in the wind currents around an overpass; playful crows and nesting crows. The baptismal Paloma. Rocío's strange lizard tail trying to distract her murderer cats. But there are the anniversaries—Dizzy and Tía Amor—Kayla's best friends—Meg's memorial service. Lent ends and Y is suicidal in my arms, eleven and tortured in fucked up legal limbo. Y whose mom changed her name from Guadalupe. Y who wants to go home. I'm not full of rage, exactly, but wave after wave, wave right on top of wave is wracking, wrecking through me. Something like furious protective energy that I'm hopeless to apply. I'm shaken and shaking. Chiwan thinks that I take sick that night because of it, that after he rages he always does, that Judeth always tells him.

Ana I worry about but I'm also holding a serious stubborn faith with her, she is one who survives.

I walk to Joanna Newsom and it's the best I've felt, possibly ever, at a concert. I listen to Plague Vendor's new album and it's like the magic of mirroring and matching. Something meets me where I am, wavelength-wise, parasympathetically, and I'm calmer, better in my skin. My skin isn't at such wrong angles to my air all of the sudden. Sierra Nicole is outside of the Orpheum; of course she is. We're still connected; of course we are. That's some witch shit—yes—if what I mean by energy isn't (as I fear) the '90s new age bullshit, but is instead a set of descriptions, reality grammars: energy is parasympathetic nervous systems. Witch shit is taking awareness (observation effect in subatomic particle etc.) to the turning, looping step of action/movement— any act, any move, sensical or not, is a willingness to listen and or change. Acts of care affect reality for both self and others. Somehow this extends to prayer; somehow spell homework and prayer are the same.

Look at me with those eyes
          not those other eyes

[30] Yesterday I read *Humanimal* and it wipes me out, wipes out the ideas of the book. Today ravens, and all along, all these corvids are raven, unless these crows are larger than life in California—it's like—more ravens here, right? Than there? Also: the concept and word: flock
Today at the reading I stand and a woman beside me sits. I can look down and see her eyelashes from above. They are tangled. So many images from the reading, this night.

The aerodynamics of bird flight have become more and more apparent to me. There are shapes I recognize. The work the wings do, their strokes in air. I feel the near-twitch in my own forearms and wrist-palms. And shoulder blades. It's the same flinch forward as watching Olympic Trials. It's my butterfly over anyone else's.

So flight is most like swimming in water. No wonder the most a body I've ever felt been is stretched into my length and using the shape of the water in my hands and around my skin to propel ahead. Fly forward, if you will. The butterfly most of all; the control and intensity needed for the most relaxed of swims. I'm an animal, I'm animal in water. (That fucking jaguar in the pool gif oh my god.) Man and women receiving received body

corvids

Crows hide their nest building
Crows show off their best building
look: shiny brilliant
up at the height—birds at play.
playful crows and nesting crows
another a pinion missing gap, close to the body.
Crow women.
Crows.

These there are the not crows. The birds.
Today ravens, and all along, all these corvids, have been ravens

Crows at all times, and or ravens, don't learn the difference
except close up

March

In like a lion; the cold lingers. It was just leap day, it was just the superbowl, it is still lent. The garden knows of lent, the flowers tease from green buds, the jasmine explodes. You weep at poetry in a science classroom. The children politely photograph each other.

March 6- the yucatecos line the streets. AKA laurel de indias AKA Ficus Microcarpa- little fingers ?

Little bone little body bleats and clucks

We ate all the shells of the sea.

We flew to the other coast: the humid heat inhales us, as if the world took us into its mouth. This is how we die. The palms, the palms. A black bird with orange crinolines. A song I've never heard before.

Flame Violet AKA Episcia Cupreta AKA Silver Skies- dark edges, Rorschach patterns. Bumpy sometimes like dino kale. Little red blooms peek out from these.

Peace lily AKA Spathiphyllum. A flat version of the Alcatraz. The flower, not the prison. Imagine the prison had been called "Peace Lily". Imagine, Imagine. Spathe= leave. Persistent leaf. A Spadix an obelisk, a tower of sex. Eater of filth. Cleanses the air of benzene and formaldehyde.

Rhapis excelsa Lady Palm, Sentry Palm. Rhapis = needle. Petiole. Saw-tooth. Inflorescence, a cluster of flowers at the top of the plant. Leaves are glossy and ribbed. The fruit and the flower fleshy. Also, what CAN'T rhizomes accomplish. Sheathed and exposed stems.

Coleus. Pink speckled hearts. My mom loves these. Once at the Home Depot, a lady started telling my mom about the Coleus all over her house in Honduras. Women talk to my mom and I stand slightly behind. I am the daughter. My mother calls these flowers Cara Sucia. About ornament: it is the devil.

Snake Plant AKA Lengua de Suegra AKA Sansevieria trifasciata AKA the sword of Saint George. A tiger's tail. Tale. Old wives actually know a lot motherfuckers.

The ruins of Tulum. You realize how old your mother and father are. How limited their movement. They are good sports, they don't want to spoil the girls' holiday. You stop under the shade and then there is no shade. You head toward the sea. The largest structure, your mother knows. She smiles and drags her index finger across her throat. Altars.

Nearby, Cenotes. The underground bodies of water. Limestone bedrock.

The shore is roped off because it's a turtle nursery at the moment. You picture the wide-eyed crías. And then the diving gulls.

Midmarch. You look and there it is. When you come back you see it the green buds on the London plane trees and the sweet gum trees near Occidental college. London plane: starfish leaves that curl up dry from the tips. Sweet gum, a kind of California sycamore, a maple-mimic like the viceroy wishes the monarch. Slender trunks, deep ridges of bark.

Tía Amor died last year.

Dizzy was hit by a car when we were in Oregon. Fuck.

I intend to borrow the trimmer. Instead, I am letting everything get worse.

March 20 The equinox. Almost out of the woods. Tomorrow the day Maura died. You sat in her room eating flowers. You sat next her petting her forehead while she moaned and whimpered. She said "Quiero entrar, Quiero entrar." You are crying now, saying this.

March 22 the day Donaciano died. Sitting up, his chest clenched and he knew. He said, "Señor, recíbeme en tu ceno."

Good Friday. Malle's father died today. Alex found him in his chair. Blood under his nose. Malle whose real name you didn't know was Lisette until you were twelve. Malle because Nono couldn't say madre/madrecita, which is what Elisa called her. (Madre: A ti clamamos los desterrados hijos de Eva. A ti suspiramos gimiendo y llorando en este valle de lágrimas, o clemente, o piadosa, o dulce.)

Other people's fathers die. You stand in the doorway and beg: not this house, not this house.

At the wake, the swimming pool where you almost drowned when you were seven is full of brown leaves.

Out like a lion.

Tulum

A wall to weep at
be the wall/the weep
water on limestone bedrock: *wells or pockets or stifled sobs*
the place of ruins swarmed by descendants and not
(decedent the dead/descendants the survivors).
At the place of altars your mother
drags an index finger across her throat;
pearl of occident on the other coast (the orient of a broken compass),
the dizzying fauna: iguanas the color of ash (as if hiding in plain sight)
a black bird with orange crinolines
and a song you don't know except you know
the roar of waves the sound of sacrifice
your mother's laughter.
Strangers point with cameras and distant tongues:
you pose in front of the temple.

Perch

You know as soon as you know
corvids know accipitrids play coy
the difference between installing/putting/sewing:
to install as in a motor, an appliance little whir little propulsion
a heart's beat a muscle's twinge
to put as in a space vacant
as in you put something over there
and now there is a gap where it was before
to sew as in surgery or dolls' clothes
corvid sew/unsew accipitrid put/unput
are we hawk do we prey/are we crow do we know
the body except for birds her body never mine
(we both wrote about the Jordan maybe
we should go to a river I would get all the way in).

Snake Plant

How tongues lift as hands
then bodies
the sword of Saint George the dragon he slays
a pen, mighty
instrument/animal
sharp like a pen, the body
how like tongues   (de suegra)
speaking/wagging sharp telling
the kind of tale in which you
do not make it but I do:
old wives know a lot motherfuckers.

Sentry

Here is a passionate dislike for riots
(meekly translated as a disturbance of the roots)
what can't rhizomes accomplish?
saw-toothed, and inflorescent (a cluster of flowers, pixelated)
the rhapis, a needle; sheathed and exposed stalks,
for indoor amusement and as eater of filth.
The sentry takes away the sins of the world
(have mercy on us/ can you see my ribs yet)
always a lion
never a lamb

[1 April] pigeons

[2] humans, ones I avoid, ones I seek, ones I miss

[3] the small brown bird

[4] the *raven* with the missing pinion, wheeling; recognize there are a limited number of birds
or—?   outside, mourning doves.

[5] that crows are the watchers, see the dead, that they carry and cross us over
step back and forth over the line
or line the line / know and mark delineation
delineate death
that's in a storybook / fiction
outside, mourning doves

[6] white butterfly (soft color, soft wing)
floating and flitting the way it looks still and hover-y then to have blipped a leap: quantum
yellow butterfly: Macondo (soft color, soft wing, petals)

[7] the big shouldered raven on the ground, approaching the sycamores; the cooper's hawk flying
at it, turning it away; their flights, air engagement, torsion—again with this blinking in and out of
vision, position, quantum scrimmage, wings, revolution from one on top to another. An alternate
universe version of the balustrade pigeons' spiral matrix tornado grace—but—the shape is besting
the raven, taking the fight to a rooftop away from the nest. "Their nest is in those sycamores," the
man says, Anthony, who is working on a project across the field from me and the stand of trees.
The hawk, cooper's hawk—tail feathers fan and the patterning of cream white and velvet brown
stripe across, stripe laterally. I learn the name from Anthony, take it and it clicks in with me. Next
to the memory my father gives me more than once as a child of watching for the redtail hawk to
pass beneath the direct sun and show red; glow; illuminate

—the hawk lands and makes its call song. Clear even though I've never heard any sounds like
this before, the variance of note and lilt and inflection; the bird-voice that carries and resonates
through the open space of the fight. (More than a skirmish.) Battle? Hawk making known its
vigilance, its strength and talon-ness, its savvy which will best the raven's and keep it besting as
long as necessary. A victory of protection. Celebrating and unfurling its hawk deeds for every
raven in ear distance.

The raven goes back to the six palms. The hawk does a flyby through the nesting sycamore and
settles to its lookout (says Anthony, "that's where you'll see them") on a telephone wire routing
pole, no sycamore leaf obstruction, clear view across the quarter mile of field and building
airspace to the palm stand and surroundings

[8] before the rain really kicks in, as the close sky starts whiting out too, the raven with the
missing pinion. There's a smaller gap in the feather line of the other wing, too. This raven has
faster wing strokes; not exactly frantic, is it working hard to stay aloft and gain its momentum?
or is that just the way the water is hanging in the air today already? there is a sense memory or
a parasympathetic muscle spasm of swimming strokes with an injury in one side of me, or two
injuries that are one per side but not in the same place, not balancing me or feeling right. The
need—compulsion—to compensate.

Late, dark, on the walk from Eva's to tacos, and back, and then again leaving, her front porch and steps have so many snails. Big ones, meaty. I am warned too late and squish the first one, twinge across my lower back at the sound and knowledge. As I leave I forget to look out for them, I step right on top of a big one. Underneath the arch of my left foot, a round shatter-crunch and soft give. The feeling of it stays under my foot all the way home and I don't rub it away in a foot bath before I get into bed. The wrongness is physical

[9] today children in Chinatown. Most knee-high. Some thigh or hip. Uncanny durability of such small frames. elasticity (of being) that doesn't snap

[11] the possum, clear color in the morning light black, white, grey; pink. Flipping away up and down—put me in mind of a rabbit, a wild hare, puppy. Gamboling up the curb and under a fence into a yard, purpose

[12] Peacock. Three bunnies, not babies but must have been born months ago—really? don't they get big faster? sitting and then scooting out of the street. Peacock again; the ancients must have seen blue, known and named it. Even more resonant than lapis lazuli, this sheen

[13] Cooper's hawk skimming east along the top of the flood control dam, closing up. An air current, or cushion, skimming at speed. It's sudden when I notice my huge debt to other women, other books in this work we're doing

—

After that I scatter. April images, shapes and vectors: The Great Horned Owl; Ravens and Crows; the Great Horned Owl and its owlet.

Looking up the Cooper's Hawk for its call, "a series of 15-20 *kaks*." A sonogram (shape notes). Accipiter cooperii. Uncommon. Open woodlands and wood margins

Still, the hawks aren't the ones I see playing in the streams; it's the ravens. Their fingertipped wings constantly calibrating their angles to the wind. Profiles become solids; shapes, bodies.

Hummingbirds come back, but not in color and barely in sound. Few amazonas—red-crowned parrots? from Mexico as escapees?

The corvids at my work have been recognizing me a long time before I realize it by recognizing them—it takes the gap-winged one three times before I see it.

All the crows have nest pieces and food in their mouths; all of them have a direction.

—

[The Great Horned Owl Day] I know it sees us. We're up on the edge of the dam, me and Robert the dam controller, using his binoculars and I know it saw us soon. When it opens a wing part way—to get some air? it's the heat of the day—I'm struck not only by its length (55 inches the book says! this one is surely even greater) but by the width and breadth of each wing, massive and powerful, each strong flight feather perfectly in place for its silence. It is so tall—and the book says 20 inches but that must be wrong, this bird it is so big even so far away down below the dam in the sycamore at the top of the dry arroyo with its streams and pools of muddy water. No crows harassing the owl nor its owlet—at least a foot tall, propped up in a little foothold on the gunnite in the shade—giant feet, fearsome claws, and yet clearly the baby, still growing barred belly feathers, maybe not flying yet Robert says.

Large eyes in its face disk. Turning its head. Made to see in the dark and we're in the heat of the day—blinding sun—and I know it's seeing us. She, I think, so big, imposing if she—though she's so far away.

The book says: Owls' large eyes are fixed in their sockets, so the entire head moves as owls shift their gaze. All fly silently. Females are larger.

—

[Echo Park Lake Day] Rocío and I walk it once, and I most love the blackbird babies and the Canada goslings. I try loving the adults too, mallards, coots, white ducks, but the closest I come is the cormorant. Rocío says it doesn't have the same oils in its feathers as the others to make them waterproofed so it must dry itself with its wings stretched out. And sure if the cormorant doesn't take a tree branch and open wings around its body, open to the wind.

There are hawks and hawks, felt as a power of summoning. Thought—hawk—look—hawk. More than once, and once there's flight I don't look away.

At the lake there are turtles and I love them too. The goslings are soft, I get the giddy need-need to touch and crush and squeeze. The human babies are mostly still or milk drunk, flaccid in strollers. I get pictures of Jude from Amy and he looks less like a sea creature and more like a river bundle. It won't be long before I want to dig into his cheeks and thighs with a grapefruit spoon and chew him. Think of biting into octopus chunks, butter firm and sentient succulent. My faraway heart baby—toddler—goes back for open heart surgery number three. Her cold clears up in time and she comes out of it well except the fluid in her lungs they need to drain off. In a week she will go home and in a couple days she'll be asking for watermelon but for now it's caught breath in the suspension, the rare intensity of unknowing when it's cast into sharp relief.

We talk amor de cuervo. I want to know, to see, crow babies, raven babies.

[30] At the marsh—Bolsa Chica—I see snails. Everywhere snails are I look I look and there they are. Hundreds clung among stalky plants. In the dry higher banks, everywhere, never have I seen or imagined or heard of them this way. I want to stop and look sitting still and take the hours to reach perception of motion / movement direction. But if I do I'll slip into snail time and my mind pulls me along, wants to be back in scatter.

Rocío sees the osprey first and then it's the only shape (solids now) to see. The rabbits are distracting—I mean focus me out of the shattered attention—especially the little young one, especially the one with the split at the top left ear scar, especially their fearless cactus battlement homes. The osprey, though. Preys only on fish: rabbits are safe; there are fish in Bolsa Chica. "They hover high, even 50-150 feet up, and plunge." Sometimes their diving completes under the water. Long wings. Dark wrist marks. Plumage white below, dark above. "They flap more than they sail, except when migrating at a height." Wings in an arch... their flight profile recognizable "at great distances." We don't hear its call: "series of loud, clear whistles." Pandion haliaetus.

All the while I'm watching for the pigeons, which I know are doves, every last city-dwelling building-nesting one of them. Rock doves, columbia livia. All coo. "A dark terminal tail band." Wing tips collide on take-off. Glide—with wings raised at an angle.

The jellyfish at Colorado Lagoon—the one without its tendrils; away from the others.

The great blue heron at Bolsa Chica—ardea herodias—nesting in neighboring palms—non-native ones—with an alarm call: four hoarse squawks—repeat and repeat.

The black rail at Colorado Lagoon, sleek underwater like a streak of swimming dolphin. The stingrays, one tail chopped off, in flagrante delicto we guess.

—

Remembering the great black and white rays 50 meters down to the bottom silt in clear ocean behind the break just west of Mazunte, and the cold fire of adrenaline determination, persisting through each upheaval of giant heavy wave, almost out, then turning to see Emily caught, not going to make it, her panic; instinct somehow turning me toward her and not away. Still loving my friend from far away and still wondering if that night had come later what might be. Breathing the one gasp the set of waves would give us together; diving as far as we could below their roil; timing the surfacing for the one breath, diving again. Fleeing. I don't remember how we touched— hands? torso?—only the connection, only the distance to the beach, only the point at which I had to choose for us beach or open water for safety, splitting the distance between the two. The way I decided. My force of will for her taking my survival out of question and into certainty, bodily yes. The stark beaching knowledge and terror that yes I had saved her life, which meant she was drowning, which meant she could have died—surfista that she was—which meant I could have not saved her. Was that real?

The surreal southern light beauty—brute force sunset glory—the night before or after. Clinging afterwards to the utter calm of the before. Those rays, that bottom ocean floor.

—

[29] Not lemons anymore. Jasmine. But it's not filling, not heavy, not weighting us back into our bodies. Like gasoline fumes never strong enough to satisfy me. I can't see the color in the jacaranda. It might as well be wisteria purple, for all that it doesn't shock me, make me real

—

*the book language is from the *Golden Guide to Birds of North America,* as well as *Lives of American Birds*

mammal

children
knee-high
thigh or hip high
uncanny elasticity to be

a possum, a rabbit, a wild hare, a puppy, three new rabbits

a sea creature
a river bundle
to dig and chew
biting, firm and sentient

Different flesh.

blue, known and named muscle
balancing bodily yes
shatter and crunch
soft give and
unfurling
and lilt and inflection toward and not away

Splitting the distance.

[April]

[*The author has warm eyes. She smiles and points a document at the audience. We understand this as directive: document. The audience observes* (and also with you). *We attend.*

I attend to the humming world. This is a source of great pain. I may have cried more times these few weeks than in the last five years. It is entirely possible. The day is my favorite kind. Cold and gray.]

[Fool's day]

Along Figueroa, yucatecos in plague season. A spotted grease coats the leaves. The workers are gentle with their tools, as if the yucatecos are extra sensitive. The warm day, the wind that is pulled through the vacuum of the tall buildings. People with lanyards.

[*that is a chair/that is a table/that is a miracle/ that is an ecstasy*]

The natural world disappears and there are only people and their extensions: clothing, tote bags, books. Their voices.

[*When people talk about the big bang theory, they really want to imagine Los Ángeles without Mexicans, without Indians and or their descendants. What silk road what Marco Polo what carnage and slave girls (we must understand anytime we distinguish slaves as slave-girls we are complicit in the access to their smoky thighs their thin wrists in bangles.* **Esclava:** *When I am an infant I get a tennis bracelet and hoops in my ears. When I am school age I get bangles and again at thirteen and then fifteen, gold, gold to wear, to show that I am valuable that I am valued)*]

Back home: the death of the jasmine, the triumph of the nasturtium

Little Big Horn: how to approach a river; stand in the greasy grass at sundance time, on the bluffs, pretty shield. No white whales for leagues and leagues but they say someone had it coming.

[**Saturday Chinatown**]

If I could marry a plant, I would marry the bougainvillea. It seems like an attentive lover. Spiral down the steep drives of Silverlake.

Night: the rain, an umbrella swinging from my wrist, a good parking spot, a short brisk walk and we see Chiwan. Ana says: "Rachel looks like she's up to no good". We wander the town looking for dinner, avoiding the places with whole carcasses hanging in the window.

Maple and 33rd (that is all).

[April 3rd] a wake a graveyard the freeways. Luis Parra from Nayarit. His brother weeping. The plants are made of fabric. I can't look at Malle. She consoles me. I feel like an asshole about it. *Remember when I almost drowned in your pool?* We laugh because I didn't die. *Remember the dismembered crows in your grandma's front yard? Remember the whole block was in Maribel's and Martha's Quinceañera? Remember we were flower girl's in Nena's wedding?*

[April 10]

Fever last night? I can't tell anymore. 3:30 am Jaime, full of glass.

After the reading/after the rain. The boughs droop; they haven't learned to stand up again. I am having bees: one in the peach branches, one in a pinched-looking poppy.

The calico on the pineapple guava and then on the roof. The pineapple guava is blooming: red fringe/ little waxy fibers that will fall and make a carpet on the path.

The ice plant stands up but is in trouble with me because it hasn't given a single bloom.
A gust of air shakes the avocado I'm standing under.

I miss Ana so much all of a sudden.

Sunday the sun comes back strong.

We wash the curtains, the sheets, the towels. We wipe the counters and the walls. The calico is holding a mangled grasshopper in her jaws.

You were writing to me and then you stopped.

[April 11]

The road workers outside. The noise of stuff. The world two days after rain. The ache I feel.

*

The sage needs attention.

The pear.

The gardenia purple/white.

*

Even a month ago it would be dark at this time.

The sun is west and bright. It is hitting a little spot on my right check, killing me, I just know it. The yard is cold.

Since AWP, basically since March 30th I feel… I want to cry at everything. I want writing so bad, I want poetry so bad. Want to unzip it and get inside and live this way.

*

The meth seller next door is speaking tenderly to his little dog, calling it "munchkin butt."

A red car.

[April 12 I think?]

This looks like October the light/the breeze.

For Rachel: a heron, a pigeon, a skunk. Not all of these alive.

[April 13th- Wednesday.]

5 am wake up

6 am begin to drift off

6:30 the calico want breakfast

6:45 the calico wants to come back into the bed

6:55 you just fucking get up

Upright oregano. The cilantro wants to flower. The coreopsis is a heathered blob. The lettuce bed is full of weeds. The white bougainvillea you got Ana for her birthday last year is doing well. With any luck it will cover her window by August.

Fig leaves, big enough to cover shame. The briar rose flush with red. The tiger lilies approach. How did an hour pass?

Are you afraid to have me in your house?

[Mental note: don't fuck this up]

[April what.]

6:30 am

Slight chill. The datura is ancient/ dead branches like deer antlers. Baby birds somewhere. The jacaranda on the corner.

I am afraid to see Jaime. I've seen him beat up before. I wonder how it will be this time.

I am constantly aware of my lack of hunger because it is unlike me and it is alarming.

[Thursday]: when am I NOT tired. When are you NOT anxious. You said *what were we thinking was going to happen.* I didn't think that. I didn't think. I didn't.

[The last days are missing.]

Enta/On'tas

The restless mind along Figueroa
yucatecos in plague season: a spotted grease coats the leaves
workers are gentle with their tools, the warm day bringing the death of shears anyway
tall buildings draw a wind, warm breath
through the narrow vacuum, the yucatecos play coy
what coyness is learned: a shudder, an uneven shoulder
cover, withhold, flutter, wink
inside the buildings a black magic muted
you walk with skin on fire (a restless mind) seeking heat
speaking canine prayers: *chair= miracle, table=ecstasy*
flush at the sight of people and their extensions: clothing, tote bags, books/
lanyards in the place of mouths.

Esclava

(when people talk about the big bang theory/ they really want to imagine
Los Ángeles/ without Mexicans, without Indians or their descendants.)
What silk road what Marco Polo what carnage and slave girls
(we must understand anytime we distinguish slaves as slave-girls we are complicit
in the access to their smoky thighs their thin wrists in bangles.)
When I am an infant I get a tennis bracelet and hoops in my ears.
When I am school age I get bangles and again at thirteen
and then fifteen, gold, gold to wear,
to show that I am valuable that I am valued

An Appalling Whiteness

The road workers outside, noise of a world two days after rain
How loud a sage a pear a gardenia in purple and white the ache I feel.
How to approach a river to stand in the greasy grass at sundance time
on the bluffs, pretty shield
The death of a jasmine the triumph of a nasturtium/
No white whales for leagues and leagues
but they say someone had it coming.

Saturday Chinatown

Up to no good, the poet wears pleats,
the poet carries an umbrella
whole carcasses announce themselves
here is sacrifice, after the rain
a bee in the drooping boughs,
one in a pinched-looking poppy
graves pinch closed somewhere, saving themselves for later
except the hollow now opened, rude a sinkhole when there are guests over
now a table now a chair, then a miracle now an ecstasy
when am I NOT tired. When are you NOT anxious.
You said *what were we thinking was going to happen.*
I didn't think that. I didn't think. I didn't.

Nightshade and what (Enta Fen)

Three thirty in some haze of reason not yours
a boy you love, full of glass and concrete
what wails if not sirens if not women's mouths
what keening and lulling, a clouding gentle heather of sleep
to close the flesh is a needle point of devotion
a stitch in time, they say, saves no one
all this talk of youths in revolting in the slight chill
the datura sheds branches like deer antlers
baby birds somewhere. The jacaranda on the corner.
I am constantly aware of my lack of hunger.

On Strangeness

You were writing to me and then you stopped.
How did an hour pass?
Are you afraid to have me in your house?

[May] shine, luster, sheen, gloss, iridesce

The matte of Poe, shadow, the flat dimension shape, became solid and then—How many times did no one tell me the story, no one even read me the story aloud. But raven, crow, turn black and get every color

Redheaded, red streaked wrens and sparrows

Person topping the hill over the northeast tunnel under Solano Canyon

Shouldered raven

And *then*: Corvid, dive play flight, front-ward-back-ward. Kayak paddlers in river eddies, features, falls

Buteos: Soaring. Circle and steep dive. Robust body—ha. Nest in woodlands, hunt in open country. "Call is a high piercing scream"

Fat fat hawk

Ah but that raven playing against the wind. At the top of the Griffith Park hill, where the wind—strong and steady everywhere all day—is channeling up the side and pillowing over the cut of the hill. Dip-diving throat first, then in a quick twist flip onto its shoulders, still diving and surfing, then back to front ways then back to back wings.

I didn't know it could be like that. I knew it played in the winds but not like that. It's worse than stabbing giddiness this time. It's WANT from under my chest cavity, a clench, a spurt, a drag of sensation down the inside of my back.

—

It rains hard and floods the street down through El Sereno. That's the day the jacaranda purple surges out of the background. Before, they were there and purple, but didn't blaze or iridesce; I counted them on the way to and from work; I tried to get back where they'd been burning icons. It took heavy gray skies and high water. This year they glow, cool, simmer. Not matte nor pastel—intensely solemn—a pull instead of a push

The week before, Rocío gave me a newspaper clipping about jacarandas she kept for me from last year. Time has looped? Wonky, lopsided

—

Yesterday I read *Humanimal* again and Bhanu writes these passages where her *I* is doing something *alongside* the other descriptions. I'll find an example. This is in other books of hers as well, *Schizophrene* and *Ban; Humanimal* is the one that shows to where I want to understand. Here is the river; these are the colors; I do this action. Describing not from above, almost not the same I writing the description. (No wonder Jen has been teaching documentary poetics; these these.)

How, though, are her actions not catching up to themselves—does she not bend and touch without thinking *After this I will write what I did*—how can it not catch up and break her out of that spell presence?

Writing this book on purpose. Writing it while writing it. Bhanu does throw the book in *Schizophrene*—thinking up a metaphor and walking across one are not the same as following one through. Your body is not expecting the way a mind can. I do not mean it does not expect, only that it expects differently. Do the thing. This is one reason we don't write only in our heads

—

The jacaranda thing: Not that bright lighting, purple and awe-full in Milano, jagging up from the earth, with Maureen

They float and smudge now, oil pastel, slipping in place

Some people in the article don't like them: There are too many, they make sticky messes, when it rains we slip and fall on their petal fallout circles

—

Two hummingbirds. One when I'm entering a door. The other when I'm crossing over to exit.
The color under jewel tones, the blacker, matte-er green and magenta. Softened feather velvet, dark, restrained
We're still here. We're at the (your) going out and the (your) coming in. Each does a couple flybys before attending to their own business, conspicuously and conveniently right nearby

[A foto of mapmaking when Rocío makes a workshop with Traci and Cathy. Not plants and animals but rivers, mountains, and place name history.]

The sweet there is is bittersweet.

Hawk after hawk. Both cooper's, on the wind, and redtail, perched.

Saturday and Sunday didn't go out of the house, save the hour going to see Yijia's exhibit. Her photography—the one called The Landscape—I've been thinking about it since then, that one, and her two others with an avocado and a persimmon

of how things feel on one's skin

The knitted-together-ness of hand bones
Phalanges which means

The thing about sense of place indoors rather than out, for the first time? The thing about the driving, cliché but who the fuck thinks I care, sky and road as constants, literal ones. That zing. [Solid shape recognize solid shape.]

The raven who sits over me, whose shit I narrowly miss. Three crows playing fighter jet formation

Before: Pigeon flight and pigeon tail feather beauty
And: Redacted
Also: How thinking the writing much differs from a hand writing. Much as thinking the prayer is another thing besides praying it—saying it rather than composing it—utterance

One time, and I'll never fight* this   *forget

The airport day. I don't see even pigeons in the early morning. The man who drives me there, we talk

In the morning I keep running my eyes over my grandmother's skin. I don't touch and try to feel how the muscle stays to the bone even as the skin loosens away. Everything hers is my mother's everything my mother's is mine, except for what's not hasn't been

The pelicans (three) can you express their glide over and on the air currents forming and shifting from the waves, breakers and tide alike

Sandpipers, of course

A white egret up to its knees in ocean Atlantic sand, dry white silica giving way to wet brown grey silt soft, then the broken seashells erring down into their sunrise palette of oranges from red to white

Lizards always and everywhere in sound and flicker

The big lean dog with white fur and playing all over everywhere

Big—big—bird of prey. Feathered thick and close to its body. Look at the profiles but you can't find its head

All the lakes. My mother's body swimming across Lake Virginia. GP loses the word for pier, dock. Then it comes back. Oh surfaces

The camellia from my great grandmother's garden outside bedrooms, the house of Harvard Road.

Shining black vulture, still on a fence pole
There are so many holes in the fronts of our face

Bagpipers processing into St. Andrews, my mom's eyes shining and my grandmother's, and Julia's face really beaming and giddy

Rings on her fingers, white gold and five square cut diamonds from 1950 what? Yellow gold and ten diamonds different sizes spangled over the textured surface from much later. Spots on her skin. Spots on hers. Spots on mine. Her eyes in her head

One shape repeats in Orlando: the high bird soaring with the forking tail. A tern? A frigate bird? A kite? I see the silhouette on the Great Florida Birding Trail sign before I follow with an icon. The Swallow-Tailed Kite. "The most graceful of all North American hawks is told in all plumages by the striking black and white pattern and swallow tail." Plumage. Then there's skin and there's plumage. "In hunting, drifts along slowly just a few feet above tree tops or low over the ground with outstretched wings and tail in constant balancing motion."

"Graceful on the wing, capable of swift flight and effortless soaring; hover while hunting. They do not dive (stoop), as do other hawk, but slip downward, feet first, to seize their prey before swooping (kiting) upward."

Elanoides forficatus; Length 21 inches; width 50 inches. Sibley knew every North American bird by its shade, by its tilt, by its habitat, according to the Audobon Society.

"Striking in its shape, its pattern, its extraordinarily graceful flight." Again without the Sound and Color, yet again the song's opening plays through. "Hanging motionless in the air, swooping and gliding, rolling upside down and then zooming high in the air with scarcely a motion of its wings." If it hunts low, then the kites were so high for pleasure, for the joy of it—immediately I realize there are other reasons: the lay of the land, the information in the wind. "Extremely maneuverable in flights. Takes much of its food without pausing."

Kli kli kli while in flight
Kli kli kli given while in flight: Yes.

Osprey "formerly classified with other hawks but now placed in a separate family of its own… very distinctive fish hawk…almost worldwide…along coastlines, lakes, and rivers."

Flying over the water, too. Two kites and two osprey. And the Spirit of God was hovering over the waters—plunging feet-first—rising heavily from the water.

MUSCLE WINGED.

Always with the bird bones, the brittle fallen pinion shafts, the dried out calamus, unzipped barbs, unoiled feathers. No more. Feathers sleek and sharp tuned to aerospecifications. Meat muscled from breast to wing. Tail gland giving its preen oil.

Pigeons and doves, woodpeckers and quails, no such secretions. Dust baths in cities, sand baths in deserts and playgrounds alike. What's a querr call?

The osprey takes flounder, smelt, mullet, bullhead, sucker, gizzard shad.

On the kite days I'm driving, being driven, through the places my maternal family has lived in Orlando. The story when my mother swims across the lake, three years old.

On the osprey days I'm swimming, delight in the water right at the break. Atlantic Gulf Stream May temperature—warm enough to forget—sand and waves gentle at the moment. The osprey up and down the shoreline where I am, north out of sight, then south out of sight, then back.

What My White Grandmother from the North, Who Married My White Grandfather from the South, Said—Driving With My Mother In the Neighborhoods My Mother Grew Up In—Orlando Attendance Two Weeks Before the Mass Shooting at Pulse

703 Sweetbriar Road
Built for $21,000
Fred Merriman built it in 1959
Phone number Cherry 11732
Cherry was CH. It was long distance to Winter Park
Mean little Mike Williams lived on this street
But there was nothing but orange groves on the left

Oh look they enclosed that breezeway
Yeah doncha know, whatshername would bathe M, she was the cutest thing, her husband was at the Air Force base. What was her name?
I can't remember. It'll come to me.
Well, we had Nancy and she was the one who M said, "Are you black all the way down?" I always had white help at home. I thought you never had a maid, Mother? I didn't. Well when I worked. They were more like babysitters. Mrs. Carter, she practically raised Kingsley. She adored Kingsley. How did you find your help? Through people, I guess, I don't remember.
Well maybe it was the Naval base but he was transferred. She got the biggest honk out of M when he said that, she thought it was so funny, she told me about that.

M pulled all kind of funnies. And like when you were at camp, Kingsley was in the sixth grade and we wouldn't let her shave her legs at Camp Tonawanda. We went to pick her up and she was wearing knee socks. And he came running to say she shaved her legs! She shaved her legs? You made me grow them back out, that was mean. Betty Jane Mann got to shave her legs! He was just getting back at you for how nasty you were to him. Kingsley didn't want a baby and she didn't want a boy. M was hard to break. One time he pulled down his pants went right in the yard. He was so proud of that.

That's all right it's just a plain old lake
And the house that you're looking straight at is where Bull Jones built
And Alli smoked like a stack
Falling down drunk

Lake Virginia where your mother swam across the lake
Fleet Peeples was the swimming teacher, he taught everyone in Orlando how to swim.
I was three
I don't remember
M went, took lessons, but he never did swim across the lake
Kingsley was always independent

That was a mistake
Yes it was

What did Mrs. Henry used to say about him? Well I thought there was something wrong with him, I had his eyes tested, I had his ears tested. But he was just immature. His birthday was December the second you know.

I think the hospital's up further.
We had a time finding it but somehow we did.

Mema and Pa.

Because it was Larry and Charles were born, and then David. No I was I'm older than David.

There's the Albertson Public Library. That's where I found out John F. Kennedy, the president was assassinated.

And Betty Jane Mann went to St. Luke's, but I was not of the in-crowd.

No you're thinking of Andy and Kitty, I mean Andy and Maud.

I lived with Grady, and then she got married, and took the car. And then I lived with Jackie. All the parents in town thought we were really racy

I called my mother and told her I needed a car. Mom went, and I gave 'em $500 on the car, and I paid Alvin Ruxter that house after six months.

And that monkey puzzle tree is still there.

One time, and I'll never forget this,

That was Hilbert and Viola's house.

2879 Roxbury Road
And we had all those citrus trees, they're all gone now. But I remember one year we sold all our oranges for $70. To a packing house.
$12,500 in '54. Mr. Folsum knocked off his commission.

219 East Harvard
Mema always had camellias, she had all kinds
Two houses east and it would have been paved under for I-4
She had all kinds, variegated, red, pink
What's variegated? More colors, more than one. Streaked, I think. The one left is white.

corvids

Shine, luster, sheen, gloss, iridesce.

Sierra's Poe matte shadow, flat dimension
shape became solid
Raven, Crow
turn black into every color

Shouldered raven.

Corvid dive
play flight
front-ward-back-ward
paddlers in air river eddies, falls and holes.

Raven playing against wind.
At the top, wind—steady all day—
channels up, pillows over the cut of the hill.
Dip-diving throat first
quick twist flip onto shoulders
diving and surfing
over again to front ways over again to back wings.

I didn't know it could be like that.
I knew it played the winds but not like that.
Worse than stabbing giddiness this time.
WANT from under my chest cavity
a clench, spurt, drag of sensation down the inside of my back.

Raven who sits over me, whose shit is a narrow miss.
Three crows playing jet formations.
Men or Women or Them.

mammal

done with bones
done with cracking out marrow
done with skin
done with sucking blood to surface
coming to muscle
coming to tendon, ligament, flesh muscle and teeth in it

back teeth, cleated molars
biting up into and down into
sinking one's teeth into
and keeping them there
relaxing the jaw and easing the pressure
leaving them gentle in their own marks
wishing almost to lose the teeth,
again have hard smooth ridges,
gum the muscle,
to *teeth* on you

bees and

Camellia in her garden
(Two houses east and it would have been paved under I-4)
She had all kinds, they both say,
but this is my grandfather's mother.
Variegated, red, pink—
more colors, more than one,
streaked.
The one left is white.

Account to me the smell.
Whipped butter and sugar
over green broken plant stalk
Sweet and pungent, my mother says.
It perfumes the car
an invading aggression
an infiltration that hits high and middle in the sinuses
recirculating in the cavity right on top of the front teeth
under and flanking the nose.

May

The sweet there is, is bitter

Feel is on skin

Solid shape recognize solid shape

And redact:

I can't remember.

It'll come to me.

pelicans

Three glide over and on the air
forming and shifting
waves, breakers and tide alike.

I want to be.
Twos, threes, and fours over the ridge of the break
at the rest where it's smooth.
In flocks for different flights, sevens, tens.

Well out to sea
in a single file, flapping and gliding in unison

Not flap— need a sound without the hard a and more ffs instead of pps—
drafting one another, waves of air
shaped by waves of water—
surging in the early way of that word.

Not a one diving splashing and eating.
All the times this time, silent.

Span of their wings
spread apart the tips
tips up or down to precisely steer
nearly skimming the surface tension
feather light adjust glide flight
then measures of lift and down stroke.

Muscle winged.

And the Spirit of God was hovering over the waters

[May]

May Day

A mirage is either a swimming pool or a march for workers' rights. You come when called; your mother and father send signals of smoke and you come.

In Pico Rivera you laugh with Maria. You started your periods the same year. You summoned the dead when you were twelve. Her boys watch Grease and sing in the background. Maria tells you she saw the mother cat of your calico. You feel something that sounds like but   in your ear; no one said it.

Only yesterday you stood on sand wearing your shoes. Rachel without shoes. You freezing in four layers, her shoes in her hand, her hair tied up.

What is there: brackish water. Brown pelicans. The geese with their elegant masks, shouting at you from the edge of the path. The mother in the nest demurring. An egret, the busy sand pipers. The orange yarn moss. The low creeping wooded stems neither of you can name. The dying eucalyptus. They are rotted at the bottom, their bodies (trunks) are afflicted with ashen pox. No canopy, no heads at all, like all the dress shops on Broadway/ headless brides. On the worn path and in the cactus overgrowth: Tiny brown rabbits. Rachel cannot. She says to all the birds: oh, you're so proud, aren't you. You're so proud.

And then: the osprey. Falco haliaetus, alone in the panionidae. It's only predators are golden, bald or great horned.

[May 2]

Grade for days. Near Otis, the Ballona creek, the houses that killed it. Near Jefferson the waves of tall grasses before the water. Clouds of yellow and purple. Then the landscaped drought-resistant traffic islands. It looks like the flayed god of spring.

What to do about my wilderness. Refill the pond, the water flowers are sad. Kill the lettuce patch. Try again. The lily of the nile gave up, cut its yellow blades like a doll's hair. Borrow the trimmer. Maybe.

Rites of Spring: a prom

An orchid, a white rose. Everyone else had velvety red roses weighed down by baby's breath. Isaac was easily four years younger than you. Miriam wouldn't come, so Isaac did. Jasmin was there, jet black hair in two high buns like a Bjork video. She wore a lipstick the color of your monthly bleeding. Her skin was so white. You forget what state her father was from, but her mom was from Jalisco, like yours. Jasmin brought Erica who painted her mouth black and mussed up her red hair so she looked like she'd just been fucked. Maybe she had. Jasmin held you for that last dance, an unlikely slow-tempo Madonna. You cried into her shoulder the whole time.

And like every single time, you say the thing you oughtn't.

[May 7]

Snails on your parent's driveway. The morning always greener when it rains. You wish for home with the calico on the porch and the bougainvillea dripping water in their suggestive way. The pepper trees swaying over the freeway. A Junco= Palo Verde, says your father. He says that when it's full of yellow blooms the tree hums with bees. You wish you were that tree.
A blackbird. Long like a mockingbird but shiny black/blue with yellow eyes.
The fields: not alfalfa but forage. What is the difference? The low wheat. You father brags that on the other side their wheat would be tall and ready. As if the field still belonged to him a little. As if he owned anything at all.

Valle Imperial: Álamo trees. Date palms. Maíz de Pollo. Onions in burlap sacks. Bee boxes- white. Alfalfa going to purple bloom. The Desert on the 8 to Arizona. The bottoms of clouds as if looking up at a glass surface.

The road narrows, the white peaks of the All American canal. Álamos everywhere, juncos. You sleep in the adobe rooms father built when he was a boy.

A Mother's day

The head of a small echeveria, peppermint patterned mini roses, yellow freesia. Sweet peas in fuchsia white and purple.

At the café a dark man and his dark boy sit next to you. (we) look like a family portrait. my mother reaches into her bag for her phone. For a second I think you think she is going to photograph (us).

Echo Park

Those apartments didn't used to be there. That didn't used to be there. Were those crepe myrtles there?

A bus with an ad. A child holding a gun.

For Rachel: A little sparrow/ a stained glass window.

Scott and Echo Park: the purple fountain grass I planted is still there, but not the sage, rosemary or lavender. In the back I planted bougainvillea to cover the wall. There was a sick lemon tree with heady blossoms outside my kitchen with the window that didn't open or close. I planted star jasmine outside my bedroom window. The girls would always ask what it was. I had to reach across them to open the window.

Vernon (here you are you)

At the library, indoor tropicals with waxy leaves. Someone goes around and wipes then clean. You squeeze one and it screeches as you run your two fingers along the blade. You instruct the room to map the body, to transpose the body onto the city. You make a map of a body that suffers cold, that burns with desire. Dendrites rise from your arms for touching. There is no touching. The field of care that is your arms. Your teeth chatter. You unfurl your brow. You always look angry. This is what they say, anyway. The sharp points in your back shudder with cold. The navel contracts. You take inventory of your injuries and scars. There is not enough death anywhere to kill you.

Communion Season

What you remember: *hunger.*

*

The thing about the body is dressing it. White, as in an injury. Eyelet, lace. You are happy to be veiled, to take the body into the mouth. You are eight years old.

Where in the body is that memory?

What is it they say? Kill adjectives? Or adjectives kill? Either way, something dies.

Garlands

A namesake sings about garlands, a lifeboat, a port. A singer who is not the namesake conjures a familiar voice and sings about hard love and dead mothers. A twinge when your name is called, a name that floated over the sea before you ever lived. The song La Guirnalda, the summer days in Cudahy not drowning. Your mother's friend looking at you like she knows you and that your life will be difficult. She has only ever been kind.

Sometimes you and your mother laugh together. Sometimes she calls you the names of her sisters.

At the concert she touches your knee and says esta tú la cantas bonito.

It is likely that I was conceived on the sea of not by it.

(what day/ no day)

All the gray days. The aloe a hydra, or those digital images of hurricanes named after women.

You get on your knees in the wilderness. You pull weeds and turn soil. Tabula raza/ when is there such a thing. Everything has consequences. Everything.

All of a sudden: Pilár Ternera. The refuge, un inframundo de carne.

A Plant nursery. Water floods the mouth. What was it the puritans used to say? Ornament is the devil. (garlands).

petunias/cosmos/dianthus

Petunias: related to tobacco and deadly nightshade. The datura and her trumpets signal dreaming and death.

Cosmos: from scrub and meadow. Leaves like bronchioles. Angelita's garden when she still had one. Remember her attendance. The palm that fell, the calendula, her citrus grove.

Dianthus: glaucous/spicy: what hybrids do. Tiny kites.

A Project Garden

Fat tabby on broken tile. The amaranth weeping over everything. The guava, pears. A place that speaks your language. You say hello! hello! I KNOW you! And you and you. The mind feels an unfurling like ferns. The mind wishes for the proper emoji.

Last days

Everything is mouths.

Decoration: bruised thighs bruised ass bruised chest bruised knee bruised ankle

And then Lent is a photograph

Eyeliner morning. You tried to say goodbye but she's not listening or she is and is saving it for later. The room is one long inhale, a held breath of three people or more. You are always the first one up wherever you are.

On Slauson is the fair, loud with banda de viento. On 60th street the palms and the willow sway with calm, the rosebushes shudder with the spring. The Virgin's procession traps you and you sing soul of my soul/how lovely you are. The pilgrims approach and you get out of your car. People come out of their homes and say her name as she passes. Someone hands you a yellow balloon. The wonder of the swarm/the terror of the swarm. You film with your cellphone. You finish the rosary. Your grip loosens on the string. You open your hand. You hear your mother call your name.

Bolsa Chica

Only yesterday you stood on sand wearing your shoes
Rachel without shoes /you freezing in four layers
her shoes in her hand, her hair tied up.
What is there: brackish water. Brown pelicans.
Geese with their elegant masks, shouting at you
orange yarn moss (girls sleeping/ girls feign sleep)
low creeping wooded stems neither of you can name
(what use are names/and what names are called)
A dying eucalyptus an ashen pox.
(all the dress shops on Broadway/ all headless debutantes)
*

And then: the osprey. Falco haliaetus, alone in the panionidae
(Rachel observes)
what names apply, what ungodly hour to take attendance
the neblina not rain the raptor perched on the dead tree
like you, its only predators are golden, bald or great horned.

Vernon

You instruct the room to map the body, to transpose the body onto the city. You make a map of a body that suffers cold, that burns with desire. Dendrites rise from your arms for touching. There is no touching. The field of care that is your arms. Your teeth chatter. You unfurrow your brow. You always look angry. This is what they say, anyway. The sharp points in your back shudder with cold. The navel contracts. You take inventory of your injuries and scars. There is not enough death anywhere to kill you.

For Rachel: A little sparrow/ a stained glass window.

Communion Season

What you remember: *hunger.*
*

The thing about the body is dressing it
white, as in an injury. Eyelet, lace.
You are happy to be veiled
to take the body into the mouth.
You are eight years old.
Where in the body is that memory?
What is it they say? Kill adjectives?
Or adjectives kill? Either way, something dies.

Garlands

A namesake sings about garlands, a lifeboat, a port.
A singer who is not the namesake conjures
a twinge when your name is called
a name that floated over the sea before you ever lived.
The song La Guirnalda, the summer days in Cudahy not drowning.
Sometimes you and your mother laugh together.
Sometimes she calls you the names of her sisters.
At the concert she touches your knee and says esta tú la cantas bonito.
*

It is likely that I was conceived on the sea of not by it.

A Project Garden

The mind wishes for the proper emoji.

(what day/ no day)

All the gray days
the aloe a hydra, or those digital images of hurricanes named after women.
You get on your knees in the wilderness. You pull weeds and turn soil.
Tabula raza/ when is there such a thing.
Everything Has Consequences, you said. Everything.
All of a sudden: Pilár Ternera. The refuge, un inframundo de carne
a plant nursery, water floods the mouth.
What was it the puritans used to say? Ornament is the devil. (garlands).
A nightshade trumpets: here is dreaming here is death
scrub and meadow (feather/fern, the paradise,
the citrus grove in the desert, a mirage):
the haruspex takes attendances
as hybrids do.

Ornament

Decoration: bruised thighs bruised ass bruised chest bruised knee bruised ankle
*

Bruises appear where there has been   *cataclysm*
blight/ bloom
flood/drought
the landscapes marks itself
to remember the blush of pleasure
of small suffering
a swirling hurricane
and blood rises to the surface to say
here was the hand of God
writing a psalm
both giving and taking away.

My Other Country

A desert east from here, south from south
what is a border but a line in the sand
my other country/ flayed god of spring
(what to do about my wilderness)
*

a grove during the enchanted hour:
In May you faced the cotton field and pulled hot oranges from hot branches. The
haruspex commanded it, your hands burning with flesh, pith. The bitter smell in
your hair, smeared on your bare thighs. You believed you were asleep, dreaming of
eating oranges, the heat was so intense.
*

The workers cutting azahares/ the wild oils loosed
the wild language of my name.
My mother wore azahares in her hair
when she was a bride, as brides do.
In my other country- that body, a desert, a place of longing
the haruspex compels= winter is delayed, the spring approaches early.
A compass, broken (what witches' hammer) points west and north
By cartographer's incision
and home is a body
a country is a body
a body of course is a map
a map of course is a poem.

Casa Ajena

Yellow dress yellow house from when you had only one language
too tall for that pinafore your hair braided backwards
someone put gold on that girl before she turns heathen
but too late, she is already speaking to the rooster
to the bougainvillea that hasn't even arrived
(what uses are names anyway/ your name the dew, the spray of salt water)
father teaches you the names: that flower is someone's prison
that vine, good for blooms, the palo verde full of bees
a junco's yellow blossoms humming with daughters.
You remember a field of fireflies is a sepia blur:
from tall grasses a yellow house waves.

Procession

On Slauson is the fair, loud with banda de viento. You think of that branch of that tree. On 60th street the palms and the willow sway with calm, the rosebushes shudder with the spring. A Virgin's procession traps you and you sing soul of my soul/how lovely you are. The pilgrims approach and you get out of your car. The wonder of the swarm/the terror of the swarm. People come out of their homes and say her name as she passes. Someone hands you a yellow balloon. You film with your cellphone. You finish the rosary, the coastal love song on Slauson ends. Your grip loosens on the string. You open your hand. You hear your mother call your name.

[June] finish May in the dark.

GP, always when I am with her, skin, and ligament. Texture and luster: Newspaper, carpet, short fine hair; clear shine of skin, of nails, eye whites. And what? Kingsley my mother's body between us.

The pelicans I can't touch how their fingers feathers finger air and water waves. (Airways.)

Rocío listens when I try and explain about the TVA flooded Appalachia and the inherited right to be ferried over to the family burial grounds on decoration day, and talk about a family deracinated (*and deracinating*), roots down, roots up, roots returned. (Arrancar, Emily and I obsess.) About regional geographies but not an accent like a waitress in a diner that tells the creek valley her family grew up in. (Diner breakfasts with my dad, listening to him, singled out accent fascination.) I listen when she tells about the North her parents crossed to, and the North their parents came to, and what her North is or was and could be.

Last year we went north together to see Amy and stay on the river, north that Amy returned to, some of her family from-there from there, and others on at least their fifth migration in as many generations. Arrancar, Emily and I became fascinated with that verb and spent all of the time after we lived in Valparaíso trying to grow roots and then trying to understand what we'd done by that. So I converted to plant attendance and mammal questions. And this is what happened in May, I could have been succinct, I could have waited for the words but instead I tried them on and off: In May the jacarandas dimmed, which meant my eyes, at first, but mirror mirror can't be all that attendance is, so. Shift around and listen, twist what you see, differently.

Pigeons. Pelicans. My mom between us. The crossword puzzle GP and I burrow into and yet both of us know she's trying to notice her own brain changing and I am too. How in all of this the *sisters* things are being said by Rocío but mine are too bedrock to write them in and call attention where they are next to me. Not wanting being a bird for the bones or air anymore, but for the muscle and the water. Not sure about animal skins. (Amy's poem.) Jude up north growing fat and safe and happy through their fourth trimester.

Skin because sugar, because anger and sugar heat link in my body and May ends with C who shuttles back into the system on Friday, greets me with a loud cry-out of—crows—my name, and launches to hug me and I hold on. "I have court next week." And by Tuesday tells me "I want to get a transgender change but my dad won't let me." I ask if there's still a lawyer—yes—another chain of facts rattled off—"If I'm in foster care I can get it" but in court C won't ask to be placed in care—"I feel like I will, I can't betray my dad"—I know about the case files that follow C around (push C around)—but I don't know their gender pronouns and in another moment the conversation ends because C's energy bounds ahead in another direction and I can't, cannot, love, but this system is so wrong and there's no effectual goodness from this seat. I'm so angry. I go numb without noticing and wake up after midnight: C loves their dad and their dad loves them and all I can think about is how old children are.

The log is becoming the work and the notes for the work feel precious or studied even when they don't feel that way but it's a new admitting, that I'm writing what I'm writing, that the notes know they're the work and my hands stay in view of one another.

May really does end in the dark, for three nights in a row I read for hours in bed and only move when it hurts too much not to.

On June 1st I open Welligent and C has been discharged to another facility by the court. (Facility, facile, facil.) Raven, cat, hummingbird, lizard, bee. Rosary of attendance.

Bhanu's writing on twitter and the cadences of Zoë's reading and speaking voices wound up in my too-open, too-dry sinus space behind my nasal cavity, and I must be learning from them and from tumblr's *this is deprecating, therefore I must be a thing.* Laying down the words I have, sometimes all of them. Laying down the words I wait for to distill on their own. How to write and how to live are, ask, the same questions, attendance...Or *is* it? ("This is a family show...or IS it?")

Tavi's *Rookie* letter this month does magic for the way it makes acting in a long run of a play twitch loud in my body. Is it even necessary to keep repeating, "in my body," the way we do *in my mind*? "I thought in my mind ____" Where else does sensation...sensate? It'd be more unusual the other options to call attention to.

To write without constantly, compulsively drawing attention to the fact that you get how naked your compulsion makes you, and someone upstairs drops something on the floor. A door opens and closes (ugh all of them so hard to open and hold open in this building) and a voice is in the hall that sounds like a man. Somewhere else are bare foot steps, probably towards the bathroom and into bed. Rachel posts again and I cry too because it hits the place.

[3] House finch—Carpodacus mexicanus—and the too many ravens article. Sycamores on the Solano Canyon hill—where are they drawing their water from? Rocío told me the name. I know about sycamores, they're almost as bad as willow for needing the water.

[4] Hike from the cafe with the avocado sandwiches up to the Observatory (jaja get it?), all six of us. Jane and I fall into step and I ask about summer. She and Tess will drive down the Blue Ridge Parkway. I say, the Folk Art Center. I tell about this Attendance and she tells about Woods, Fields, Town. When we approach the lip of the hill, the first hawk is up high, slow wheeling against ravens. It's so big. We are in thrall. Powerful wings and filled out round in his or her breast. We start pointing out and the hawk—redtail we say at this distance, what else could be big enough?— stops on a high branch of a tall tree. There's the other one, Jane says, look. And the other one is guarding the nest more closely, looks like. Their shapes are solid flesh, warm and pumping. When the first one pushes back out into the air, we can see the entire underplumage. I haven't seen one so big, and its tail feathers didn't show off pink. A golden eagle, that's a big enough bird, more like 32 inches than 20, 25. Jane also sees the raven playing in the air, the one who flips onto the back/ wing top. Jane sees a lot of things, including her opening shot: a wreck of a building, burnt cinder block and cement poured over the town; then the dissolve—the old growth forest.

On the walk down the hill, India tells the family secrets story.

[6] Ravens and ravens and ravens. We—me and Rocío—work on a project description so we can give it to Chiwan to run excerpts. The ouroboros stresses me a little bit but also makes everything feel REAL which also stresses a weird part of me that wants to know things are real without validation at all.

Remember that thing about corvids demarcating the death / life / death lines? Holy / awful? These ecology prophesies? and by prophesy I mean describes reality. I mean a Sign, signs. Revere, as in *vereri*, as in the place you stand when fear, when awe, when respect, when bow. And guard, as in ward, as in tender, keeper, watcher, protector.

January hummingbird mistletoe: try so hard against the compulsion to say I KNOW THAT'S ANDROCENTRIC and wave that knowledge like a flag to protect me from being read as unaware BUT it feels way more new (I almost wrote Important or Necessary, ugh habits I ugh at) vital? life-ly? to write stripping off the blankets of comfortable awareness-that-exempts. Expose and then—is it shameful? is it a moment among many, like and unlike? Mistletoe is how it *felt*. I've never kissed under mistletoe. I remember my stories, isn't it a bit of a curse to be ware of?

Redacted. And emotions are thin loam and clothes are so uncomfortable but not to be wrapped in something is unbearable.

[8] Today was really weird. Yesterday now, since it's 2:30 a.m. Ravens.
On foot, bus, train, carpool, vanpool, swimming pool, carpool, train, foot, car, rental car, foot, vote, foot, bus, movie, bus, foot.
No hawks until car down the 110: Same sycamores, same stretch of arroyo, same hawk? In the air, redtail fanned out pink light through.
Squirrels, sounds of hummingbirds.
People all day less sound than sight. More shape and space.
Put a soft shirt on already, lay you down to sleep…

[9] A cockroach crushed half smeared and surrounded by the small ants.

[10] On Friday Alice came with baby S to swim. We haven't seen each other in weeks. I can see how she walks what she means about the back pain. It's good between us, always, but we aren't there together. Until we go in the water. We are different after, connected again. There's a lot that doesn't need to be said but it feels weird to skip past it.

The bird—one of the fast inquisitive brown ones—the one who is always up by the wading pool. It—they—skitter on the surface, back and forth from skimming the water to shaking it off on the rail. Alice points out the chlorine could hurt it. The bird seems careful and quick. That same joy bolts through. Is it bird joy or only attribution? Movement, decisive movement, could be some of joy. Hurts good.

At night, as the gathering drifts, we witch. Rosemary in the corners, breath and heat and urgency. I mostly follow you while I'm struck all over again by how powerful you are. Lightness too, in the recognition of your intensity—in your cat family—in nerding out—if there is a way to be a nerd and a witch, you are. Like petals, you text in the morning. I wait until now to write back: like the haboob. August 2003, up on the hill behind El Paso, roiling back on itself, irreversible, awe-some, stunning, covering the outskirts of Cd. Juárez and then the center and crossing the seven bridges and upon us, nothing in our bodies but thrill of fear and thrill of joy.

[11] Next morning, orchids from Jessica. "I was going to get, I meant to get purple. I saw these yellow ones. They're soft, softer."

The little birds will be the ones. The raven flying over on the backs of its wings, all gristle and pinion.

The kite, swallowtail, shape and no solidity. This small, this palm of the hand, this cupful of color. We keep saying, brown. Brown bird. Brown sparrow. Brown wren. The colors of brown. And another gift I can't believe.

[12] rain. How much blood in one spring? Answer: more, always. *I don't know.*
The small brown bird, bright on the crosswalk sign, peeking over. Pigeons, palomas. Go. To. Bed.

[13] On the way back from the vigil I see a rat on the next corner I need to cross to, moving towards the angles of a man about to step into the street. It is a black plastic bag.

[14] The ones with the red heads and shoulders, and brown and white striped breasts. One brighter and redder, the other burnt red-orange. These times I stand still for as long as they do, show themselves.
On the drive, two redtails, one light pole apart. The first faces south, the next faces north. They are, they look heavy-chested, but now I wonder how much they really weigh.
Later on the route, a sharp-shinned hawk, from the size and the shape of the tail.
Pigeons on—Maple?—another holy ghosting, tripled. Afterwards the undersides of the wings show. Every pigeon paloma in flight with their special curved angle skims on flashing dove white. (Did I see it, or did it appear to me—Meridel Le Sueur again.) (Damascus, what is it all about?) The whites of their wings.

[15] One pigeon on the balustrade, turning from the east in circles.
Up on the hills over La Tuna Canyon, two ravens fly the pas de deux / wing-slip instead of foot-step?
No hawks
No snakes all year; no snakes since the Sespe Wilderness, which means 2012. How??

[16] Whittier Narrows, we go on a field trip.
Redtail hawk: Giant, powerful, pink in the tail fan
Presiding over the field-warren creatures (prairie dog cousins?)
single solitary flight signaling many doors and intermingled lives at illegible
The further and further spirals towards high-horizon
broadsides of wings approaching the view, then slipping to slivers and breaking the limit
A long time longing: to not be nice, to never be nice
Sharp-shinned hawk: skims and darts. Striped all across the underbody and ruddering a sleek right-angle tail.
Cooper's hawk: swoops and lands up in sycamore canopy. Still and aware in layered cool green. One wing refolds and not a display after all. Lost to sight, out of vision field, no movement.
Two stands of sycamores over, their calls pass through open heat
You make their call, have learned it now from their distant cousins at Raber Street. Strawberry milkshake, chocolate milkshake, small ground cover green with small orange soft flowers. You see the last hawk, mouse in talon, supper. The hawks are big, maybe too big for the bird book dimensions. A trifecta at an all-you-can-eat buffet.

Missing phone calls at night, two staccato text messages.

[17] News. Missing phone calls mean *phone calls* and I check in with Nicole at 8:30 in the morning. The news isn't good. Alex and Nicole tell me what we know so far. Later, at LAC/USC ICU Unit 5B, I gather that there has been a cough. No corneal reflex. 40 bed unit. How many hours everyone has been there. The characters of nurse, resident, attending. The bathrooms for visitors are often occupied. How swollen with fluids our bodies on life support. Lack of cell service on the 5th floor except near a window. How long until family arrive. How many surgeries so far. Alex's body and mine seated side by side, taking turns doing the leaning and matching up, taking the steadiness of

next-to-one-another-ness where it can be taken. The medium gloves run out. Use the large or the smalls. The medium gloves are refilled. Count the times you sanitize your hands, once for every entry, once for every exit. There were two hawks this morning. Weren't there?—?

[18] Santa Ana: Making with hands. Convivencia / sobremesa. Rocío and I compare notes on Spanishes and Englishes on the last leg home, after we greet Jen's two cats. Not many pigeons. Odd-clean, locked-recycle bin, bland tan brick kind of place.

[19] small dogs want to snuggle and you want to be left alone?—? Failing to (lacking—missing) attend. "Present with..." "Hold space with..." blank. Blank with.
Sunday, Father's Day. Walking up the high end of Alta Loma, a cement smooth retaining wall head-height over the sidewalk. (Always, the other retaining wall, along Lorena between First and Chavez; stacking overhead high.) (Mission creep/body creep.) On the phone with my father, actually. A snail on the wall, and another, wait—the heat and dry drew out their slippery life. What Is Left: Amy's first name for her manuscript. Dry shell, dry glue, and at some time, soft sound splinter, smooth carbon, weightlessness.

[20] Summer Solstice—San Gabriels
Mourning dove coocoohoo c-coocoohoo hhoo hhoo hhoo
Full on daylight before the sun anywhere near clears the ridge
There are four, it turns out, on wire above the bedroom window
Two and two. No know how many or who were hooing
You'll come later with Ana to take attendance.

Summer Solstice: The sun pulls all day. Hummingbird in the tall orange flowers. The moon sends us to sleep. Somnolence. No more height energy, all drawn out and now gone. Warm and drained on the (ir)radiating concrete/road, sidelong bodies; not a gentle glow, no. A shape-shift moon, or moons taking turns in quick succession, not getting lined up exactly right so we can see the flaws in the flip book panels.

[21] Raven in that one shade conifer. Throat-croak-warble? Percussion on light hardwood? If croak mean something more like croon. Clocking tongue is the closest we do in our mouths, I think. Perhaps song. Part of the day is this sound, listening for it and sifting it through words. (Remember that thing, "gem-mining"? Sluice and trough, silt, rough rubies, between crumb and pebble.)

Too, the pigeons outside the dark hospital seem to be their own tribe: different flights, different rustles. Same as the rest with the white, though, bright underwings. Not luminous glow. Not gentle in the night, no matter how warmly I tell about my day, no matter how deep the breaths are (regular, regulated), no matter that I only hand sanitize five times and my knuckles don't dry this time. (Still tar or another carbon in a thick deposit inside your right hand.) The size medium glove box is full.

[22] right now it's not living wrong I'm concerned about, it's dying wrong.
Hawks, hawks, then this heat, smoke dissipates, none.
I take the youngest two classes swimming, all boys, fierce bodies, easy soft ones, tiny muscled ones. Keep teaching them to float. Kicking and breathing. Then float. Again. One of them, tension bound and not an inch of fat to help, loosens. Eases his shoulders and neck, floats even. Relax but a different kind of relax. I also teach them to pull each other to safety without falling in themselves.

The high pitched noise is gone before I ask if anyone else hears it, too.

[25] Meg's story about walking out to see the garden: "Is everyone still alive?" "Are we all still alive?"

Scumble is a word. For her the Jacarandas were "I noticed I wasn't noticing them" this year too. Less rain, not as much purple in the tree? More rain, more color around the purple so it doesn't stand out so much? (That drought really washes you out! That rain aka life giving sustenance really kills your vibe!)

Moa messaged today. I can call her just to talk, she reminds me. Again the light shudder of how necessary to have a voice at the end of the line once every few time zones.

Attendance: "Present" "Presente" But the bullshit new age baby and bathwater appear as manna each morning and one's hands are reaching towards them as for the first time. When I... saints and feast days... today/present isn't all (just like lol phoning it in v. showing up.) Therapeutic words may be wielded as weapons. You know. This presence, the one in attendance... [illegible] sleeeeeep lol failing due to lack of attendance

[27] Hawk sparring with two ravens above La Tuna Canyon, pink tail. Hawwwwk!! Giant giant right above the lip of the and upstreaming in meandering loops. Not meandering at all; you understand. Peter and I meet and make the plan for the reading. And then Alex calls.

12:30am I come home from the hospital and there are smells as soon as I walk in the door. I empty the flowers where I left them too long in the vase water, soggy stalks. There's only one dish in the sink. I wash it. I'm smelling it in here, or I carried it home. I carried it home in my head or I carried it home on my skin. Or in it. Since a week and a half, motorcycles EVERYWHERE. Tonight not a single pigeon neither at entrance nor at exit. But three motorcycles on the drive. Motorcycle flinch in the morning. Go to bed, Rachel. Feels crass to write right now. Cindy Sherman room on my back mind.

[28] June 11:30pm still feels not-mine to write about the scents in my house when I come home. I was wrong which flowers—it's also the orchid—all the blooms browning and wilted—two as yet unblossomed. Sarah answers me, "I can be as explicit as you want." Morphine, air hunger, prolonging, most people don't go until, hearing is the last sense.

12:something a.m. Jeanie texts, "he just left us." I don't look at the text; we said goodnight. She calls minutes later. Thank you, I say. I kept holding her in her tears last night, and night before, small in my arms, tall me long arms, it still wasn't getting to me. What wasn't?

There's a bang on the door. Think of the color of the courtyard paint.

[29] Thick slats of bright sunlight cut with the haint blue pillars in shadow. Alice comes over and we talk about the next appointment. The baby wants a waffle and fries. I re-read Sarah's long replies to my long questions. "Also respirations will be 30 seconds apart right before."

30 June

skin tender
tenderizer
pigeons on the balustrade
peacock who won't speed up out of the road
if skin can be tired
if fatigue is heat between muscle and bone // layer where it should touch bone
the meat on the bone
the meat falling off the bone

[June]

[Early]

June happens in the middle. May holds on hard. A glass of whisky makes declaration. Your mouth is always ready for communion. What are wives anyway? You are not one; you don't have one. In a lair guarded by beasts, that young feeling of inexperience and immolation. You remember that year, the way you relatives became afraid of you. Here is black magic. Blood vessels, the blush of a wound you never felt. You must admit, you like the monthly bleeding.

I felt myself about to lose control

A song about dancing girls, the cold empty house. You warm yourself by wearing eyeliner; you are aware this makes others warm.

this terrible shadow

[June, now]

The sacrifice of water. Abstinence is watching the wilderness dry up. You turn away like the mother with the sickly cub. You keep walking toward some Summer. Small cries from the ground, from the old avocado and the datura feel like nothing on your heart.

Later, downtown, the yucatecos steel themselves against you, your curse of drought. You walked with bare arms down the street.

RP came. When he walked next to you, he offered you his sweater. i knew what i was doing, you said.

String lights on the yucatecos at night. The noise of mammals in the season of ripe fruit trees. Did you smell mangoes or did someone just talk about them?

RP: an abundance of I don't give a fuck.

The memory of shared breath, the ashen lavender morning, the same color in your hair a familiar mammal. You dream of running in forests on four legs and tearing into red flesh. Your thighs are red. The red swirls down the drain.

A quiet understanding, the blinking screen. You don't remember walking through the house or even the understanding. You only remember being able to see instead of the usual blindness; Animal. You could see. And then you really asked for it. And it hurt like the breaking of something. You never get sick. You always just get injured instead.

[Junish]

The familiar body, my body, what is a body. A row of saplings planted in careful rows on a concrete sidewalk. The prayer of *one day shade.*

You remember that you hate remembering her. She was never interested in plants. She did not have a familiar. But you dress to be looked at.

Attend the night- the red lights, the traffic signals as coy eyes, blinking. Pretty women show their backs to you. And inside, a garden of lights. Three whiskeys in, the room is alive.

At an enchanted hour, the drive home. The garden of red lights. (*garlands*)

[June 5]

A garden of bodies. Steam/ it's too hot to drink but Ana is so nervous she has two glasses of wine. Rachel and Ana each with their arms gathered up like gathered wood, afraid of the forest of people. The lines in her work/ the lines in her work. Works hold hands like Aspens under ground. How like trees, everything.

A girl slurred near your mouth: You dainty. You so dainty. The sides of her red smile curling up.

Chelsea Wolfe

The crab grass in the empty lot, the old yucatecos so big their roots lift up the sidewalk. Two witches in black. The blue light, Ana with her hood on.

[June 8]

Attendance at the beach. You are marked absent.

[June 10th.]

The roof: red pebbles. Or chips. Succulents. Gin, eight avocados. Gin. My black dress. The darkness crept up, the chill settled and we went downstairs

A place full of witches.

I made a net, a ball of butterflies, and thing to smash, the next day everyone had fevers

[June 11]

In Southgate, on Tweedy: crepe myrtles.

In DTLA the long-saved breath and always through Chinatown

[June 12]

You find out about Orlando late in the morning. The LA Times has already printed a different cover story. The plagues of Egypt, the sons and some daughters.

Whittier Narrows

The sunken block, the path when I was a kid

Three kinds of hawks, a buffet of ground squirrels

That time we were lost from the older cousins

The freak show

[June 18]

Saturday with Jen.

The Chinese elm in Jen's front porch, an extension of the house. Ulmus Parivi Folia. Single toothed leaves. Leathery, lustrous. The bark: flaking, mottled gray wounds. Cousins: elm, hickory, ash. For cabinets, for climbing.

The sad morning at the office. Feeling orphaned. Rachel a scared lamb her eyes big as lakes.

Already her eyes dewy. I pledge to protect, but my sorrow may drown everyone. What good am I at this when my own mother doesn't just scoop me up and say mine mine you are mine however you are.

And then Santa Ana. Drive toward heat. A gallery, a fountain. So many brides. You do not have one/you are not one. Lights on strings, on dwarfed olives, their bark. The difference in translation: right here/over here/aqui/aca.

Upstairs the magic

The hot night/the place of hot winds /of that general/the fort with the name of my father's favorite tree.

A corridor, we pushed the tables. Each clay pot spikey button cactus. The careful pots of tomato and squash, velvety leaves, like hands. The potted paradise. Succulents. Rachel suggests theft. Pluck a little cutting here and there to plop into my pocket.

Geranium: Mediterranean, cleft leaves. Five petals like hearts, propagation. "the crane" beaklike seed. Mouse moth.

Here is the north

*

You think of Lancelot, recovering a water borne sword from his mother. A boy like that, from a haunted mother. Aren't all mothers haunted? I realize I want to be haunted. You say out loud.

Somewhere, a Siberian elm/Asiatic dwarf. Ulmus pumila. Good for shade, for supporting various vines. A dormancy.

[June 19]

A father's day- cachanilla: pluchea sericea. Siempre verde Silvestre. Chozas- construcción de café cenizo cenizo., un verde grisáceo. Hojas lanceoladas "sus flores presentan un arreglo- corimbo" eyes- axles. Only things tear. Dense impenetrable thicket (thickets).

[June 20th]

Hot at dawn. Attendance at the emergency vet. The soft pink tile, the leafy fichus in a plastic pot. What wounds are. You water the yard before Coco after Coco, as if it won't be evaporated in a few hours. The thirst of the wilderness, how generously it continues to work even when I withhold water. What will become of us in this desert place. The theft of water, the ghosts look out from the high places. You feel them everywhere.

You get Coco home and clean the house good. The floor so clean and cool you lay your body down for hours and only blink awake when you think you hear your phone. Out in the world, the wall of heat. Mexicali.

During the hours of heat, I would go outside for little whiles to feel the intensity, like being underwater. I would go the citrus grove and face the cotton field. I would eat hot oranges as bidden by my grandmother. I get up from the floor and am compelled to the kitchen. I tear into an orange and eat it over the sink in longing for that other place, the place on my body that remembers such a heat.

A fire, out there/ a full moon.

Out in the world, a fire near the rock quarry, near the creek of white stone where your father took you as girls. The terrible plume of smoke east. You imagine the deer, the coyotes running away. You figure maybe squirrels, some raptors in their nests, didn't make it. You ask for stories of fields in a wild place. You think of earthquakes often; you want the rain. It seems impossibly far away.

In Altadena, the dry hillside and chaparral. We stood in the road in bare feet like girls. The moon floats up, yellow as a house. We lay on the hot driveway and murmur to each other. Wild things rustle in the plants.

[June 21st or THE TRIMMER]

Make a place to take attendance from. Level the branches. Trim the hedge of sticky blue flowers, move the furniture around. The Calico watches from the roof. Make magic. The mother(s) cast a net.

[June 23rd]

Blood to blood: what you must do is go to the healer, cartographer, to map the landscape of the body and send a satellite how inhospitable.

A glass shard party. Seven days after the cut, you will remove the adhesive, or try anyway. You have always been afraid of reopening old wounds

In the dark room eyeliner magic. On instagram. I'd be lying if I said I was not aware of my eyes. Ana returns with stories of rivers and pines. I can smell the forest on her and have never wanted her more.

For days and days you move pots to the farthest part of the lot: an old trunk we used as a table, the echevveria and potted palms. The plumeria I started from a cutting. This is my summer place. As if summer could be a place. The land of summer. As if summer was not a season in which things also die.

[June 30, 2016]

The embarrassment of survival. Between the event of death and the community acknowledgement of the event of death what is that lull.

*

Tiger lilies arrive. The rust color on my bare thighs. The blood that returns. How I like it, lit up like a flame.

A wild place/ tiger lilies

You remember that year/ the way your relatives became afraid of you
here is black magic, inky as pens (you wrote your name in blood that first time)
*

I felt myself about to lose control
*

in that dark you could see; *animal*
and then you really asked for it (the tear or break)
you never get sick/you only get injured:
arachnid blood vessels, small bursts of lightening
the blush of a wound you never felt (being born).
You must admit you like the monthly bleeding
the way the red swirls down the drain.
*

Outside, tiger lilies arrive
the rust color on my bare thighs/ the blood that returns.
How I like it, lit up like a flame.

How like trees, everything.

How like nature the shared breath of bodies,
the way aspens hold hands under the ground.
How like gossip, leaves shifting, curling, falling:
elms and yucatecos frightened of drought, of the open mouth of thirst.
They shrink from you as you walk down the street, you carry thirst.
In a wilderness, you turn away from the cries of the nightshade, the bay laurel.
Strings of light (garlands, ornament) blink coyly:
a crowded room, a forest (you dream of running on four legs)
and gathered arms like gathered wood.
The painter/ the poet gather up and steel themselves
the lines in her work/the lines in her work
willow, pepper tree withdraw and shake
(*she brings home the river and the pine/*
she smells like a forest).
You have never felt such thirst.

Brides

Nearby, the citrus groves shudder with desire,
azahares give themselves up
fall into soft piles of death and sex
brides float made of plaster/shards of glass
what are wives anyway you are not one you don't have one
how sharp that weapon/ how white your teeth
(one cannot help but stare).
When you were a girl you played the Nayarita bride
for sixteen breaths
you hurled yourself nowhere, perfect—
the others swooned and rose up with sheathed arms
touching palms folded into heavy hems
blossoms falling from your eyes
sharp teeth of desire,
your fortune a pile of salt.

[1 July] A friend of your dead friend sees a black cat pass on the street
Silent birds in the bamboo; no hummingbirds yet; a baby praying mantis

[2] You didn't think human mammal bodies would include this. The bright head wound on the
raccoon (which month was that?) comes up in the back of your eyes. You are writing "you" like
Rocío now, and not like yourself, "towards." She wrote your own words down before, *What were
we thinking was going to happen?* Your life has prepared you for this, if anyone's has. (If this is
possible to prepare for; if preparing for this makes a difference.) There have been more hugs in
the past two weeks than in the past year. Human contact. Is mammal contact different than avian,
riparian, reptilian, marine? You park your car on Friday and you won't drive until Tuesday.
Machines and bodies don't belong together. Your grandmother is sneaking out and your sister is
tailing her around the small beach town hoping to prevent an accident. Rocío's morning pictures
with Scout help. Sierra's questions—lose, loose, and loss—help.

[3] Someone else sees a black cat and I don't.
More hugs. I want to get fucked up and I do. There's swimming in the dark at the end of every
other part of the night. Well that and then fire, is how the night lasts us until morning.

[4] On the roof a big one winging south. The wings are too broad and wide to be anything but a
great horned owl in giant silent flight. But it is a body in the dark.
Later I read about the eagle that flew away from the baseball stadium. But why south, if it was
the eagle?

[6] No animals on Alameda, Seventh, or Los Ángeles in the hot morning gloom. Pigeons—
palomas—in the air over Sunset. Tails spread to land. Feathers intact.
"I've had things die on me."
No writing about the datura

[7] Such fat pigeons. Mama comes and we swim

[8] Rocío says hummingbird tiny in the morning
At the station, the train: hummingbird,
vulture/buzzard, vultures, buzzards
from Los Ángeles to San Luis Obispo
vulture, black angles, black sheen, beauty
the back feather line—
sunlights the tips—a brown shine thick lines following the edge opaque
In the fields, north, brown gold, light gold, velvet
lush and dry
My sister could have died in that car. My sister could have died in that club.
These wrecks. And behind them,
behind, ahead miles, everywhere on the underneath surface
this cauldron full of what if not blood, anger, love
a clarity that this time won't discard itself?
A condor. Giant gulls. The memory of the condor
is the deck over the cliff into the air over the ocean.
With Sarah. The stars. The biggest brightest starburst
far cold burn.
There's—
where the words went.

our human bodies, mammal creature bodies,
how do we hold each other, shield from spectacle, hold one another,
this death and grief writing and this finding actions, acting,
this gather together that changes our grief, that changes our bodies, that changes the sea tide, that
protects and serves our bodies…To revere one another bodily…I don't know.
The birds weaving wheels over Morro Rock, and loud
The tensions in my body about my mother's body driving (about Grand Pat, about Julia, about
Theandrew)
The turn of the summer into wreckage is wreckage
a trauma floor, a man who doesn't wake. Two who don't get a chance.
Run out of ink
who am I to matter my words? set that aside, that's not all writing does

[8 and 9] Motorcycle machines lined up, lining and revving, idling in a rally at night on Cannery
Row

[9 Monterey Bay Aquarium]
the tanks glasses of thick water, thick mammal and fish creature bodies
my mom comparing the rooms to meditation
full rooms of folks and mostly it's the babies and children I see but the parents and the couples
on dates, yes.
The octopus knowing their people by their skin; the octopus tucked into themselves and holding
to the thick glass turned away from us looking; soft-looking underparts staying grey-white, grey-
cream.
The jellies—their science name—disco roller lit—completely clear, some of them, at depth
without atmospheric sunlight.
What part, percentage of our space light isn't solar?
No whales. There on the deck, a person working to point out the whales and otters and dolphins
in the bay, points out the whale watching vessels battle shipping, wheeling and converging around
probably a whale but can't see if they are seeing or not. A spray which might be blow, again since
Big Sur, no whale bodies, just ex—air—forced out air with water.
Sardines and anchovies in a tightened circle circulating tank column cylinder. Otters as she
weasels, a weasel is a what is it are they like? The shark cylinder/penta-volume columns—slow
whirl life—how is death in these waters—besides what must be planned feeder deaths, krill
maybe.
At lunch we look around for a long time and think together about money, affluence, the aquarium,
the community, Disney. The environmental plastic and etc. art grabs her and I notice my surprise.
THE RAYS!! Bat rays!

[10] Golden Gate—So many fucking motorcycles—to the farm in Willets—
Rattlesnake!! Ostrich, ostrich, humans unplugged
reading under shade tree in a grouping of slouchy lawn chairs *readers reading*
Vultures, their body feathers and wing feathers, shapes, overlying, two shape overlay.
How one vulture delineates death / afterdeath as compared to? as proximate to? as proximate, as
approximate—*proximity is neither like nor not like*—Martha Ronk again
how more than one corvid delineates life and death

[11] Farm. RIVER. The Eel River, baby kiddos, body bodies. Berries with Magnolia.
Hanging the laundry out, staying in the hamaca, the dairy and grazing cows gravitate towards
me. It's not until later that I recall all those hours of translating from French, *Les Vaches*. Of

course we are looking at one another; of course they're looking at me before I'm looking at them or indeed anywhere at all outside my device, on which I'm reading away the *magical light of the late afternoon*. Walk with my mom up to the Peace Bell and ring it out. Small snapping turtle by the lake fed by the springs. She sees it by my feet I'm the one to pick it up and we are careful peering into see its/his/hers/their hook beak snapper shape face and I love it for its back feet fins diggers in the mud vicarious mud between my toes. Where I feel animal empathy* is also in my feet bottoms?

*What's this animal empathy word—bodily?

[12] up the North Coast towards Crescent City—Redwoods, driftwood
Crab—my mother!—"it's dead" so what's the problem
So many godforsaken god dammed motorcycles
RIVER. Klamath. I go back and read more about Blue Creek, salmon, and Yurok people riverkeeping

[13] Oregon Coast and a Eugene evening: Rocks, shoreline. Shrunk back. Fatigue of unattending. BIRDS! back deck with a table and then just BIRDS group attendance group attending family attending?

[14] a full day in Eugene, with beer and hiking: Mosquitos. Mosquitos.
Birds back patio: hummingbird and visiting foe—black and white woodpecker—pair of black-capped chickadees.
Harder than I thought for me to say the words. (Hike from lava fields and woods to lakes.)

[15] Driving to Portland together
Breakfast birds
Harder than I thought to hear her say the words to me
I barely looked out the window
Butter baby (I can barely write anything about what it's like to be with Amy. Bodily/present.)
Oriented by this time almost completely towards and around tuned my mother
My sisters hold me as much as they can from across the continent—I am shocked by my continual inability to feel only what my managed expectations predict
reading with Sara June Woods—soon to be Moss Angel—and FUCK: *Sea-Witch*
my mom in the room

[16] in Portland: Really a coconut butter baby
time inside and outside
nature walking path: baby, Amy's hungry, (Rocío's texts about 20 year old "baby making parts")
blackberries!!! Redacted.
Giant Raptor on the light pole between the Willamette and the Columbia
Laughing: JUMBO RAPTOR
hummingbird—Amy says—"I always / only see / notice them with you
crabapples

[17] Portland to Seattle I barely look out the window. Adam's impression of his track teammate who ran like/with a velociraptor/'s arms
Ravens ravens only ravens

[18] Seattle by the water with Angelina, during light and after rain

Breakfast with Amelia, food together, her making writing and making space and making community, now and soon

Crows Corvids RAVENS everywhere and only
Goodbye with my mother, who reads to me and asks me, from my book (mine; mine?)

[19] Seattle indoor light windows
Garden, no corpse flower bloom, but, the place a corpse flower did bloom
RAVENS called over and over as crows
Trapeze: Bodies in space bodies in time bodies in movement
(that a body could be outside movement, but that a body MOVES with inner and outer forces:
play. In the senses of joyful / mischief also: the extra rope / slack which allows adjustment and
give; the opposite of constriction—just such a rope/line is presently trapeze—safety requires
it—a motion and length which both follows and anticipates the flyer—(the sound of the trapeze
spotter's commands/calls) (up! ha!)—
PARTICULAR bodies, not this "the body" which departs from "Le Cri" into stasis)
is this, are these mammal/spirit/anima/alive I'm writing ("fauna") or has it all been an excuse
("pre-text") to write position, posture, PHYSICS
And in the past, pasts, my, and Katie, how our bodies

[20] Seattle to Oakland to San Francisco to meet and read with Chiwan
In my body I board a flight with an expired DL
in my bag is the passport Chiwan posted to me when I realized
in (the body of?) white supremacy today it was not needed (required of)
I'm not hassled I'm warmly reminded to renew
passing papers—still gatekeeping—inequitably (yet gatekeeping in essence yes inequity
institutionalized
Ravens every time tall in the trees

[21] San Francisco to Oakland to Burbank to HOME
deciding what to read later; hearing who will read
more boarding flights with two IDs, one sort of invalid
passing through Fruitvale station on the way to the train

[22] School in the day—the public transit—getting ready slow and easy for the reading
after (flute / channel / breathed) voices than mine, another and another and another and another
and another and another, other (fin / wing / moved) hands than mine, another and another
The thing of it is the Sand Fire. The maps of the Sand Fire, and later only later thinking, *fauna*

[23] smoke pool
not hooking up but cuddling a bit, cuddling some
feeling enfolding-er and bodily remembering the good standing next to the tall woman, fuerte,
forte, at the stop for the Flyaway at LAX, the guess my body was making about the sensation of
being held enfolded by her. This bigger than I taller than I broader than I stronger than I, woman.
the *twin want* gone or displaced?
unsettlement ALWAYS of a same size woman versus the settle in feeling of a same feeling man. still
a writing unadjusted (when *to queer* is a verb we're going to *use*) by the head-knowing rejecting
gender binary; when do we know what we know?

[24] dark dim comfort quiet cool and not cool

[25] Train time. The bird with the pale white pinions sheathed, long smooth, just alongside the dark gray, visible from above the body nestled wings (Paloma)

[26] six pigeons, seven, palomas
on the streetlight (here a drawing of it)
~~trading~~ places taking finance and war terms, notice and set them aside, other words come
swapping, switching, realigning their spots—
is that/would that "change their spots" ours?
(that phrase from the story that comes to English through Kipling? in the war? the one that's still war?)
palomas over the bus stop from Pasadena gold line (gold) to Altadena
rearranging themselves—or assumption—arranging themselves in relation, towards one another
/ one to another / some and some others

[27] The train—the bus, the train, the bus. On these days there are ravens and pigeons. My student—her mischief. Nona comes over for tea. English/UK for supper?

[28] The other pigeon paloma, on the same place on the walk, black sleek folded pinion folded into the gray. My student—her labels. I make a budget and think how this is a kind of Lent?

[29] Turkey Vulture—Cathartes aura
Two-toned wings black head when young
"new world vultures"
Order Ciconiiformes, Family Cathertidae
"more closely allied w/ storks and flamingos than hawks and falcons but listed near for field identification"

[End July]

The palomas flocking together in the cool of the morning (short cool of the morning) and the cool of the evening (long low light, and after).
So much history landing on July—All Stars, racing Allie and Martha—the Odoms dying all at once—reading *Harry Potter 7* with Sarah in Nag's Head—Becoming a Senior Instructor—and another ceremony a year later—*Harry Potter 7* movie with T—the storm that night (that morning)—and this book released and the reading for it. That landing a little today. So much death on top of itself here in July after June.

July

human mammal bodies include this
bright head wound up in the back of your eyes

machines and bodies don't belong
corps and carne
lose, loose, loss

human contact
I want to get fucked up and I do
swimming in the dark
the end of every other
night, that, and then fire
how the night lasts us

but it is a body in the dark
a kind of theft without names
vow intensity and urgent
fated to pluck things and grow them inside me

no animal hot morning gloom
I've had things die on me/
nothing about the datura

jimson weed   moonflowers   vespertine flowering plant   toloache
toloatzin   witches weed   poison   desert thorn apple delirium
tropane alkaloids   wasp honey toxin   photophobia   heliophobia
          death

vulture / buzzard
north to where I was born
(mountain fields place)
(brown gold, light gold, velvet lush dry velvet)
vulture, black angles, black sheen, beauty
the back feather line—
sun lights the feather tips
brown shine thick line
follow the edge opaque

cauldron of what if not blood
far cold burn

where the words went we hold each other
shield, hold, grief, writing finding
acting, this gather that changes

loud birds weaving wheels over Morro Rock
revere one another
bodily

(as opposed to careen) (as opposed to scraping)

the turn of summer
into wreckage is wreckage
a trauma floor
a man who doesn't wake,
his friends wake up
his other friends line up machines and rev

thick water, thick mammal and thick fish creature bodies
behind thick glass or plastic

octopus knowing is knowing by skin
octopuses here are soft and under
grey-white and grey-cream
tucked and turned away
no whales
vessels to watch
but no whale bodies

slow whirl life
how is death
look for a long time
together, with bat rays, skin under my skin

RIVER: the Eel. Body bodies. Swallow Rock.
Each berry with 'Nolia. Black blue straw red raspberry black raspberry
She looks through my camera, takes
as many leaves and stems as she does blooms.
vicarious mud
more than attendance, what is a bodily empathy word?
animal empathy word?

RIVER: the Klamath. Her body won't go down heights
I only have a couple minutes to take in all the blackberries
a ways down the cliff path
rocks and sand
waters meeting and making
the cool water, cool enough for swimming up, cold enough for life

shrunk back. fatigue of untending. then just BIRDS.
Mosquitoes mosquitos BIRDS

it was harder than I thought to say the words
lava fields and woods to lakes
cold fixed lava hot unmelting unmoved under the sun

RIVER: between Willamette and Columbia.
a giant raptor, a giant pestilence of blackberries to glory in,
time inside and outside

really a coconut butter baby
always only with you

barely look out
then RAVENS RAVENS only RAVENS

RIVER: the Duwamish, the Sammamish, the Cedar
Poisoned or laddered for the anadromous
/ana/ but play but laughter
by the water during light after rain
now and soon heights
crows, corvids, RAVENS everywhere
only: ask me

(play; extra rope or slack in the line; give)
a motion and length follows and anticipates
and in the past, pasts, my, and Katie, how our bodies

RAVENS every time tall in the trees
the maps of the Sand Fire and later
only later thinking /fauna/
thinking I'm not tending
not tender anymore enough

we know dark dim quiet and cool
dark dim quiet and not
the bird with pale white pinions
long smooth sheathed along dark gray

six pigeons, seven, palomas on the streetlight
palomas arranging
relation towards, one to another

on these days there are ravens and pigeons
look up vultures
cathartes aura

palomas flocking together in the cool of the morning
cool of the evening

[July]

I used to like July.

Etiological (a story of why/ of causality)

The end of June is shrouds is kinds of theft without names.

And yet: other people's mothers. The bachata and reggaetón in the background. The same blue, big as lakes.

The blue flower: plumbago auriculata: raceme/a short stalk/a spiral arrangement
where in nature is symmetry? Scoliosis, one eyebrow, one lazy eye, a shoulder, one hip, a breast, etc.

The wound on the leg is still careful, butterfly the name of closure without thread (or also of slicing open)

[Friday July 1st:]

No Mabel (the cat)

You are still away: the lair all me, full of longing. I sleep tucked into a pocket of bedding. So much room to fill with the light in the trees.

My scar not a bright red eye covered in white butterfly, now a thin red slit- an angry mouth? Unamused. (always bruised/injured)

[Saturday July 2]

6 am- las mañanitas

The song of king David, something about rocks and enemies

I smile and get up to stand in the wilderness and do not cry at the songs of my childhood:

El tiempo pasa by Ramón Ayala
Se me olvido- by Juanga
La media vuelta- J.A. Jiménez
Libro abierto- Cadetes de Linares

In Karineh's front yard- a pomegranate, a citrus, a kumquat. The paver stones wind like a spine through the gravel. The dry hot. The fruit trees stand in the heat, trembling.

That crepe myrtle is really going to town/ all I want anywhere is elms

Sit under the peach and the tree I don't know. The don't know is a terrible itch.

Faerie lane haunted, the calico so curious as if she hasn't been there before. Her little face.

[Monday July 4th]

4 am witches call, moon's caul. Griffith Park with Esther. Stand in the circle of trees, say my witch's prayer. Pray for the whole wolf clan. Pine, elm. The stones, the heat.

Jessica wants a love song. All I can think of is obsession: wild horses (in hollow bones)

Late for mom and dad's, for Ruben, his laugh

[July 5 the walk/ the laugh]

[July 6] the tower of Babel, all the tongues and laughs at different pitches.

[July 7]- lunch w Kingsley. The lakes, the sun on her skin. Her gentle questions, her deference. A smile comes easy for you, you know her.

At night: mitski at the echo/ sage. We stalk in red-lit corners. We leer from the edges. Her hands strum the strings with the indifference of blooming flowers.

[July 9]

Pt 1.
I just ovulated/I am sitting in a chair; women touch my hands and feet/the throbbing and scrape in my left ovary; I stare straight ahead/a painting of a smashed vase/or is it a bouquet flying through the air/I always want to tell someone/make a pronouncement/like the child who declares they suddenly understand/the value of the number two (two-ness)/ but who is there to tell useless information like that to/I might as well tell strangers I found a missing sock/or finished the dishes without cracking a single cup

Pt. 2
Three things I borrowed today/all I saw was your burning body/feral with vulnerability/ something about a white horse and a carriage/ a line of dead eucalyptus on my left side/ my sensible voice says they could catch fire/ and then I approach and see the ground is charred/Annie with her mom tattoo and pretty hands touching mine/ touching and all I can do is feel the molt and kick/ all I can do is stare at a picture of broken flowers and cry

I stole a plan- snapped off the purple labial succulent with sprouts- is this my fate, to pluck things to grow them inside me.

A Live Oak Hand Fast.
What vows are what eyes say. Wolf clan stands as witness. The dry field, a coyote. The jacket of an eden, the white space between flora and fauna. Earlier I ovulated sitting at a manicurist's station

[July 10th]
(a lifeboat morning then my mother's garden)
look a wolf in the face/ outside coyote pups squeal with delight at the taste of blood.

Mother harvests garlic/come vampires come werewolves lips curl in recognition of the monster the longing to walk the city as wolves

Kitten goes to the sea

[July 11]

Morning: walk around to test the soil hot damp or dry. Must clean out ledge. Little scrub jay in the peach/ other years the mocking bird drove them out.
To do:

Get glazed pot, pot the milkweed/Clean up foliage/ boards/Strawberry planter in the bushes

[July 12]

Un paraíso interior/ my landscape a wilderness I cannot map. In my life I have been cartographer. My small hands mapping my small body. mother walks in says "I'm going to tell your father" is it that day that you remember ever being afraid of her, the end of trusting her completely?

At the doctor, you are comfortable with your nudity. You quickly undress. A paper gown a flower of a kind. The doctor purrs at your perfection. How curious, that place you can't look at.

You picture your uterus (not womb) like a mark ryden painting: a little Madonna in cuts of meat or intestines or slices of cake (house of loreto and bees and ferns)

To walk down the street triumphant, unable to tell everybody. And yet, nothing has been accomplished. Except not atrophy. Somewhere in you the twinge of hope (is this possible).

I don't want (that I don't want- you switch to Spanish)

Needle- the tech looks like Lenny from Laverne and Shirley

The blood drawn- this is sacrifice. It hurts and keeps on hurting. Three vials later. The sigh shudder and loosed tears- the self care after: sushi and pinot grigio before twelve noon.

Another lover another mother maybe a mother that would love like

The truth is I never stopped thinking about a child

Unalloyed, perfect, perfection/*she purred*

Perfect: is me at 16, in costume, the balancing fire on my head

[July 13] the day my father was born

Up at 6:30; water outside

Point of concern: the future of marigolds, the alyssum.

The bay laurel: the children dying of a slow (long) thirst. You spray them with dew live goddamn you (lagrimas de cocodrilo)

Little sparrow- two male two female

Waiting for transcendence/ the blessing of the corners: Blue flames erupt in your palms, you fashion a ball of light you see your fingers as spider's legs making a fine thing. How soft and sharp a good poem is. Even when it is painful, how lovely an injury. You weep with grief at the joy of a wonderful sentence.

What a wonderful sentence/you make me feel like a wonderful sentence

And then the after, the polite helloes. Telling Jen about my doctor's appointment. Being instructed to write my paraíso interior, to be named: el vientre perfecto de Rocío Carlos

[July 16]

A Maggie Nelson morning. A fern by the window, some other potted plant. Outside, the cactus in a neat row. We slept in an uneven bed/ a soft hollow center

We walk toward a pillowy roof like white sails. Ships on the sea, a nightmare I have often, or is it a memory?

A sign for whiskey pulls us, just slightly after noon. Immediately, I'm crying about nothing. The corridor the bathroom, the gaudy mural of ribbons and cherubs on the wall, the fabric roses covered with dust.

All the while I think of you, the line of your body, the long torso and firm legs. Little bow mouth. How long until I corner. Turn a corner.

Look at a picture of a back yard / satellite of love/ and weep.

Such palms and sycamores. Magnolias.

[July 20th a Wednesday]

The day after the full moon brings me my blood in watercolor blooms, the pillowy lining arriving like leaves that fall out of my clothes when I've been working outside. Drink enough to fill a vessel the size of a pear (or is that a closed fist). When we were young and reckless you would toast to the vacancy of that place, a place which in me a doctor pronounced perfect.

[July 22] wear black, see everyone's hands. The dark bar. Rachel's laugh and light light.

[July 23rd] The morning of ash. The fires north of here. The orange haze. the smell of smoke the burning fields after the cotton harvest.

A daughter names the silence on your tongue, fluorescent at the end of green-lit linoleum corridor the hovering bloom in a dark room clean feet on clean floors hands hold onto doorways. My mother walked me to the Guadalupe in red brocade. I was to understand the heart was made for swords. She handed me a dagger and pointed at her chest. It was like a pin cushion; there wasn't room for one more. So I plunged it into my own chest. She nodded that, little witch, you chose correctly. She taught me to grind the bones like maize. And then to bleed onto them.

Ornament (2)

I rise to attend to be attended to your teeth in my clavicle in my hip how delicate your teeth fine as keys in the mornings you can't even make a fist but your teeth are always ready for me.

When you grow accustomed to her bed the nightmares come so you seek other beds each time a sorceress casts her net over you and it works for a time until the breath stops the breath is what makes the spell, you see and water always comes burial always comes but you never do.

More than just a body but be a body how could we not I am always in my body I want that, my body to fall forever, to go to pieces/ I am a witch in service of creation/ all I do is give my body to attendance, to the presence of the world/filth eater/I take it and put it inside of me/ I am the font and fire/I walk through a room lit up.

As if nothing happened at all (portal to death and life)

To a baby: The best thing I can give you is no memory. (take away the grief of happiness) The alternative is that the good days become a nostalgia, which is a wound and the other days are wounds opening and closing and opening like eyes.

[July 25-30]

A wild fig one block from Fruitland and Soto. To find it, take Figueroa to Pasadena to Broadway. Enter the 5/60 interchange and exit Soto. Go all the way down, past Olympic and the Sears where your mother would buy you popcorn and the Mormon thrift store. Past the animal rendering plant and the cold storage warehouses where your father and his cousins labored. Somewhere nearby is the sewing factory where you brought your mother lunch and met her nice old bosses.

Paper flowers

Attendance: short blue hair with a shaved ¾. The ombre in mermaid green. The soft pink waves and pink brown. The kind green eyes always on the verge. The fuchsia pixie. The queen of leopard print. Such able hands, all of these. Such voices for screaming. The black lips, the red lips. The loud bang the song on the cement courtyard the street where that first love lived, where she led you into the empty attic and you nearly died of thirst and lost your voice. Then the Ferris wheel at the spring fair at St Matthias.

And Raquel. And my Mom

[July 29] the green at dodger's stadium, the faded lawn. Yasiel Puig. Fireworks. Union Station with my parents.

The blue light at night. The lair alone. The AC. The body. Absent of song.

[Sunday July 31st]/ La palabra:

Up. Water/ bless. Observe. The house alone. Sweep the corners. Wash sheets. Clean feet on clean floors. A kitten returns with the road on her. It rises from her like vapor. Face the train tracks, the road of dust that kicks up. Across the tracks, a family plays summer jams and fills a plastic pool.

Pomegranate *for Karineh Mahdessian*

In every portrait
in the hand of the mother
or the crown of a queen (or the tombs of queens)
the seal of a covenant, a thread of scarlet.
Release the seeds
sarco testa /testa being seed
(daughter, granddaughter)
by scoring or beating, or in a bowl of water.
Tolerate frost, thirst and tired feet. Walk against the wind,
fire behind you. Fly or swim.
Hide these (daughter, granddaughter)
in the hem of your skirt and the curl of your ear.
Listen here for the frost in July,   *aril,*
amniotic,
in this vale of thirst
here, a reference to my apparatus
or the word diaspora
here, jewel of July, a reference to the dead and the living
punica granatum, gem-like, my body
full of rubies and things with teeth
(I Wish You Would/I Have Teeth There you said to the marauder)
your fist full of treasure
she told me to eat the pearls/ syrup and tang
washed my mouth in blood.
Three pomegranates falling. Storyteller- are you listening?

A paper gown, a flower of a kind

You wonder where in nature is symmetry
when the touch is touched there is touching and Scoliosis,
one arched brow, one lazy eye, a shoulder, one hip, a breast, etc.
this is the lay of a land how it lays now lay down
the wound on the leg still care-ful:
butterfly the name of closure without thread (or also of slicing open).

Interior

The day after the full moon
the pillowy lining arrives like leaves
that fall out of my clothes when I've been working outside/
watercolor blood blooms sharp with iron—
bottles empty/ bottles make music
drink enough to fill a vessel
the size of a pear (or is that a closed fist).

(when we were young and reckless you would toast
to the vacancy of that place, a place which
a doctor pronounced perfect)

A birth day somewhere, King David's song:
something about rocks and enemies something
about the cleanness of hands.

Fruto/Vientre

A paper gown holds you like rhapis/ a pistil
Of course everything is sex
unalloyed/ perfect, perfection/*she purred*
perfect: is me at sixteen, in costume, the balancing fire on my head

how curious, that place you can't look at

holy house of Loreto and bees and ferns
the fine thread of this this this

walk down the street triumphant, unable to tell everybody
not atrophy not that)
I don't want (that I don't want- you switch to Spanish)
The blood drawn- this is sacrifice. It hurts and keeps on hurting. Three vials
later. The sigh shudder and loosed tears- the self care after: sushi and pinot
grigio before twelve noon.

Another lover another mother maybe a mother that would love like

Ornament (2)

I rise to attend to be attended to
your teeth in my clavicle
in my hip how delicate your teeth
fine as keys
in the mornings you can't
even make a fist but your teeth
are always ready for me.

*

*When you grow accustomed to her bed /the nightmares come so you /seek other beds
each time /a sorceress casts her net /over you and it works /for a time until the breath
stops/ the breath is what makes the spell, you see /and water always comes burial
always comes /but you never do.*

*

More than just a body but be a body
how could we not I am always in my body
I want that, my body to fall forever, to go to pieces
I am a witch in service of creation
all I do is give my body to attendance, to the presence of the world
filth eater
I take it and put it inside of me
I am the font and fire
I walk through a room lit up
As if nothing happened at all

July

Etiological (a story of why/ of causality)
is shrouds is kinds of theft without names.
And yet: other people's mothers.

A daughter names the silence on your tongue/ fluorescent at the end of green-lit linoleum corridor/ the hovering bloom in a dark room/ clean feet on clean floors hands hold onto doorways./ My mother walked me to the Guadalupe in red brocade./I was to understand the heart was made for swords./she handed me a dagger and pointed at her chest/It was like a pin cushion; there wasn't room for one more/ So I plunged it into my own chest./ She nodded that, little witch/ you chose correctly/ She taught me to grind the bones like maize/ And then to bleed onto them.

And August beginning, the sisters and I with the parents' anniversary. Exploding? makes waves take time highway

[1 August] hawk fattened even though the heat melts
At Raber Street house, Ana calls out the pair of doves, who we don't see—then there are the mockingbirds, four, full round shapes, and in the high naked branch in the full sun heat. One flies and shows its white underwing marks. Two starlings fly together, diagonal, one vectoring and then the other,

[2] pigeon palomas and questions about birds who flock together and flocking. In general.
The bat flies in our faces, seated for Dudamel who keeps playing. The Bowl is dark but it's a bat for sure. It's eating mosquitos. My eager greeting is heard by our neighbors.

[3,   ] I lose the plot but pigeon palomas
a hawk from the train
two hawks from the car
only and always flocking together
are alone ones not of a feather

seagull a head taller than the fat palomas
in maple, the end of day debris
in the gutter, gray and white
with long legs
    not of a feather or not flocking?

murmur:
why and where more than how

with Rocío, flat of the roof,
magical light of the late afternoon
("I don't say magic hour") (Cather, prairie)
the murmuration sputter, two and one,
three and four, eight of them [line sketch]

Moss Angel, self-described den mother

last night the three girls counting their fingers and toes: how many am I holding up?
starlings: look, I think they're red, while they
in a shadow and then into light—
they are and glow—too many to count but fewer than our combined fingers and toes—

their own gyre and wheel
wider turns and higher
the hand that remains / open
(Chiwan, body skin)
loose turns at speed

fucking, and wanting narration
not wanting dirty talk promises I can't keep

Just say what is right now happening
with prepositions (*s'agir*, from Latin or from the way older verbs are the most irregular, *agere* I
think)

Bed-raggled?
Attending Eva and Damien's backyard
meeting Mali
singing into the phone with Rocío
Days and in a row of Rihanna

where is the wilderness
without a car
questioning to say
wild, wilder, at all
if not in relation to
(destructing) (man) then
to stars or tools or...

in the dream, the pheasant,
the not killing and the taking golden pheasant
feathers   the belongings packed lovingly
into half the trunk space and a   .
certainty leaving behind

Redacted

August baby peacocks and parents
?turtledoves
littlest birds in the dirt yards
orange feet palomas   flocks with space differences
with a gray white amongst gray grays
Not to breathe
Not to attend to time
Not sunshine, light, sunny out,
[is attending to time necessary to attend?]

On the roof over the bamboo thicket
(thinning thicket)
no birds then loud sudden birds before sun, dense noise from small bodies,
and then cooper's hawk. [sharp-shinned??] gristly and unkempt
or juvenile and molting into sheen, it lands on the roof opposite me,
lower and close to the bamboo birds
as if a routine stop and then to -hunt- swoop, half a dive, the smooth down and across curving
entry into the bamboo—then—no change in sound, neither tenor nor timbre nor pitch nor
density. Death
and a meal
or not death?

important correspondence / dants

"What it means not to be a danger to someone else" Gabrielle Union says this on the internet

August: last drives, last arroyo parkway hawks,
big flockings of parrots, asymmetrical palomas on the ~~over~~ strung wires

Read Anna Świrszczyńska, finish in a day *Building the Barricades*; and listen to Ashaki
rendered, rent; and renderings—the emotion A writes out of (in)—the death Ashaki writes out
of—I am my mother am I? stoic and waiting for feeling? Absorbed in an accusation of being cold
and unfeeling; but it's something *he* put on her (with the help of patriarchal church) and I refuse
to reinscribe this on her. She lives and feels deeply, why else this coping? I do too live in heat, in
human feeling. Elinor, I keep her close. (Later I will note that I don't know who I mean; later than
that I will remember.)

[18] The ducks three under the train over the river, shallow water spill from the main channel

Pigeons flicked on the light pole and across the way on the phone line.
The second time, Flocked to which first?

White pigeon mottled with gray in its scrabbling flock of dark gray palomas, in West Hollywood,
in the morning. Or where

Horses, what animals (what an animal) their encompassing warmth, heat, hair skin.
Sensible (pronounce these letters in Spanish and there's the sensitivity sounding like itself)

Datura open in the morning finally closes in the heat of the day
It was wrong before to see it open and wilting in the just after noon It's right to see it strong
vertical and waiting for low long rays
The datura must spread with night wings, moths, what about bats and birds

Downside up bird on a wire—not clinging, just hanging out. Almost perching body language
and a mockingbird—white on wings when it flies south away. The differences I'm still learning of
mourning doves mockingbirds and

Tiny beagle puppy unleashed and clean on the alley pavement just needs squeeeezing

The foto of Jen with baby Paul

Redtail hawk, redtail hawk; what is sentry?

Sleek crow sleek crow rough raven sleek raven. Crows so small now.

August

waves take time
Hawk-fattened
though the heat melts

.

pair of mourning doves
then mockingbirds
full round shapes

.

the high naked branch
in the full sun heat
I want to hide and I do

.

questions about flocking
and flocking in general
keep playing

.

a bat for sure
air weight differing flesh
in body wing muscles tendon
ratio

.

lose the plot
hawk, raven, paloma
seagull, finch, parrot, wren
only and always flocking together
are alone ones not of a feather
not of a feather or not flocking?

.

chatter birds
starlings? look
the little girls say
I think they're red
in shadow no but
into light they are and glow
their own gyre and wheel
wider turns and higher
loose turns at speed

.

fucking, and wanting narration
not wanting talk promises I can't keep
with you just say
say what is right now happening
with prepositions

.

always, August

always, most months
now—after tonight—

.

days and in a row of Rihanna
you—
needed me
and
must be love
on the brain
I used to
I could, I did, move things around in your body
feel and hold my hands over your anxiety and
approach
feel it shift places and
coax it out your lungs into
air in the back of that divey-ass bar
but I wasn't
there was no tired
of being *played like a fucking*
violin

.

excerpt from August letters:
wild, wilder, at all
under
T for tar hard in the palm of your hand—swollen; a solas; sugar-anger
for routine stop
for prayer, for papers at night
for license and registration
for killed
for hit
for fuck
for ether
for bathe—for after

.

the bamboo thicket (thinning thicket)
no birds then loud sudden birds
dense noise from small bodies,
cooper's hawk gristly and unkempt
lands on the roof opposite
lower and close to the bamboo birds
a routine stop
~~hunt~~ half a dive
smooth down and across
curving entry
no change in sound
neither tenor nor timbre
pitch nor density. Death
and a meal
or not death?

.

live in heat
in human feeling

.

(under the train over the river
shallow water spill
from the main channel
and three ducks
making their life there)

.

white pigeon mottled with gray
in scrabbling flock of dark gray palomas

.

for months the whites of the flowers stay
open to the sun past noon
by the end Datura open in morning
finally close in the heat

.

in the morning
or where
redtail hawk
redtail hawk
what is sentry?

.

waiting for long low rays
no space, no ritual anywhere
but attendance and more
its absence

[August]

First harvest. The Meyer lemons. Instructions: squeeze entire lemon into glass of water. Drink nothing until this. Put on gloves and wade into the thorny thicket with bare legs. Tug gently the stem; they are all ready to come. Notice the absence of the moon flower.

First harvest part 2: the lavender. Long stems from ferned leaves. Little scallops, eyelet, lace. Press the fluted blooms, wet as eyes. Enough to remind you of me. You are always so far away.

The memory of wheat fields

A new moon, a lion somewhere. Night ritual and prayer. Kissing her. Whiskey for the ladies. Make the ball/ net of blue. Behind you/ the stone wall. The calico stalks a skunk.

What you remember on a Wednesday is the sacrifice. A mature female, you enter that place/ wet as eyes/you lose your armor, drunk with flesh, you leave wings, antennae. *Surrogate*, you say. *Take this body and eat it.* You leave behind a brood of daughters. They will die this way too.
(you eat fig after fig and weep)

Mornings, the Morse code, the raven clicking.

Intend to write about death. Instead, remember it and receive wave after wave of it. The shudder and the weightlessness, the weight that is left after. Pall bearer/ mourner you witness and labor (and here is a document of death).

Bury me at_____.

[Wednesday 3]

open the place, be puzzled by tourists in matching green corporate t shirts. Two old fashioneds later, It is decided: pancakes for dinner the following day

[Thursday 4]

pool attendance. Rachel's *I want to get fucked up and I do*

A body in the dark

What if not blood

Spectacled

Gathered-together bodies

You revere another bodily wreckage

(that tree/the specific body)

The past/past

When do we know what we know (we never knew)

The one that's still at war/the still-warm

And Luxardo cherries

The period that doesn't come. That kind of absence.

The sun set on you/ on the roof. A couple taking photographs. Sirens on 7th and maple. Planes pass over. The craft depot where your mother bought lace.

The morning reeks of lavender. The mystery peach jojo found- you can't find it again. The pears are falling off the tree. A brutal negligence.

The new moon, the good will.

Figs wait/ birds wait/I watch

The grapes- I was waiting for them to be ready. Instead I let them shrivel up on the vine. Yellowjacket's frenetic hover.

A summer approaching/a summer in rear view

Eva's garden: is it rude to be at a party and take attendance? You wander with your second whiskey and touch leaves: That aloe with the yellow borders. climbing rose sunset color. pink tinged rose. some thorny some not as thorny. shiny avocado. it gets wetter in Tucson. how you have to think in Spanish to write it. the line. want to crush the leaves. the apricot. green. the soft spots in the soil. the banana? the hibiscus. incognito camellia. the soft purple blooms. the fig. a hidden guava. Membrillo here named *quince*.

Again trim the plumbago. The pile of sticky blue blossoms proto-carnivorous. You think of trapping things with your body and then eating them.

What big eyes you have someone says. You let the answer hang in the air between you. Somewhere, candles. Somewhere.

The tower of Babel is where I met you. There was a party. And you said the plainest thing I ever heard in the only language we had in common.

A Christmas in august where hallways smell like bleach. A potted fern. The last days of school, the sycamores gangly from thirst, their spiny children floating in spiny broods. Deer cross in front of you regularly.

Two chairs facing the bluffs and the canyon beyond the field of yellow jackets who have instructed their daughters for generations to end you. You think of your mother's sewing needles, her fine hands putting together and taking apart machinery, sewing buttons and pricking herself for your benefit and then turning the needles over to you and happily you prick yourself because this is part of it. You suck your finger and let the metallic taste cover your teeth and tongue like a film. You show her the drop of blood, perfect as communion. All of this because wasps chase you on a dying lawn.

Cover/ below in the canyon. The body is the cover.

In your mouth the name of god a tongue you never learned you are spoken to and do not speak except to say this way or that (we met at the tower of Babel).

Parrots: amazona oratrix

When the heat settles the amazona quiet you sit so still a sparrow alights and looks about.

[mid august]

The warm night under the magnolia under the magnolia

What full moons bring when a woman writes about bleeding is it always that way? I am not that way let us attend to the walls of a garden alive

Progesterone- the thickening thicker thickest /a fly paper to catch the Easter.

hummingbird/ your flutter. Prostaglandins: here comes agony.

What words are: make small things

Water features, what they are/ we worry for water

A fancy shawl dance

In Sonora (what grows): Your mother's birthday. Mother mountain range/ pearl of occident. The lazy tongue saying señora, the xeric, the halophile. You learn to love on so little. You mistake the rain for weeping.

You are a pearl, rose. No you are a grain of salt. No you are a coffee blossom. No you are a prickly pear. No you are an orange blossom. No you are a rose.

*

Shoot me she says, if I ever make anything that looks like it was made by a woman. The coy eye and wall of no. and then the hedge in front of the house is gone and then it was Friday.

A paper crown and the invitation into a girl's room. /You remember those days, pink everywhere/ a wall of pink and then the pink walls. /Is this where you remind the reader: it was only a movie/I was so young then.

And the can't get up because there are wolves/ in the snow and they are here for blood. /And there is blood.

*

A Monday/ his yellow tropical building. You walked to the Raymond and it's closed. You walk down glenarm under the myrtles. You make a plan for plants. You go the bad place to retrieve the good things. A tense guard lets us through, locks the door behind us and doesn't say goodbye.

Tuesday: again to the dark place and then up the streets with the fine homes. Dusky workers part when you greet then/ a pale child watched from a window, her mouth on a straw. Aloe, salvia, echeveria. Crocodile tears. Under the magnolia- nail varnish.

And then to the place of red light. Lanterns are like figs, I think. You stand together. When you read, you are speaking in an empty room.

*

The ace theater/the church of it/ the lights. And walking downtown as a pack. Little wolves all of us, with quick steps (from my mouth to yours/ just like a spark)

And always the train/ the sound of the summer leaving on a train

*

The end of summer

When Juan Gabriel dies. The town is quiet and then joyful and then quiet. My mother blinks with shock. I turn over all those afternoons at my mother's friend's home. Her cassette tapes on repeat: Juan Gabriel, Rocío Durcal, Isabel Pantoja. Así Fue, in Pantoja's Andalusian wail.

The wilderness noisy at night, unaware of the world's mourning, full of howls and shrieks, thrashing. My body, the wilderness. I shudder with the fighting. Late night calls at the back door- how feline/ursine, little creature. You should be careful of me, your alpha. (mothers wait under tree covers to snatch their young back/ mothers teach the lessons, understand?). The sigh and quick breath.

Another day/ the day light- all of baby paul. My small hand bigger than his little belly. Hs conductor's hands. Then home. Then dtla la cita- the lights and Esther and the platform at Union Station. I am a beast alone, walking alone. I miss Rachel.

Closing down the city for the night- did you say that to me? From another place. Did I hear that or read it?

Pyrus Communis

Temperate/vulgar the pear in flower
wet as lashes, snowy lanterns
the labor and performance and then the limp ornament,
(how common the curve of my body)
superfluous as bruised petals
what brutal negligence, fallen fruit
the cartilage as cavity/as longing
the muffled singing or buzzing of flies
a mouth left open/the viscous pearly sentence
written on my thigh
(let us adore)
another bodily wreckage, the past past
a summer approaching/a summer in rear view.

Taxonomy

In Sonora (what grows):
the mother mountain range/ pearl of occident
the lazy tongue saying señora,
the xeric, the halophile. *You learn to love on so little.*
You mistake the rain for weeping.
*

You are a pearl, rose. No you are a grain of salt. No you are a coffee blossom.
No you are a prickly pear. No you are an orange blossom. No you are a rose.

What if not Blood

Again trim the plumbago (this is not without its consequences)
blue flowers as net, as fiery arrows
hungry, the blossoms slip into your shirt and hair.
Proto-carnivorous/think of trapping things with your body
and then eating them.
Progesterone- a fly paper to catch the Easter the thickening thicker thickest
What big eyes you have someone says/ you let the answer hang in the air between you.
Somewhere, candles. Somewhere.
Cover/ below in the canyon. The body is the cover.
hummingbird/ your flutter. Prostaglandins: here comes agony.

What words are: make small things.
As if we didn't know how to say: we never knew.

[1 September] how long do hummingbirds live? Is this one on the back deck—in the California garden—the same visitation? (Five years ago I felt visited; now I feel visiting.) *you can have the body you want / this summer* equal to death

[12] raven silk black

hawk from the roof where we have our feet in the pool

bat-bat on Paloma outside Dennis' house for dinner

the ravens have their mouths full again
(change of seasons—?—change of winds)
(change of air change in air)
the sound of raven wing in air—much more like yucca Joshua Tree—the hard lilies family—than soft petal touches from soft lilies. more like pulls of water swimming than breaths on air

there were more
the territorial hummingbird more;
the flock of parrots flying over Crenshaw at the ten around 630a
at dusk ravens matte black on one face of their wings and gold bright reflecting from the other face

dead dry earth worms on the sidewalk at work

"You're a child right now"

[19] Did I say the heron? Because the blue heron, gray in the morning due west, or west-southwest, marine layer halfway up the San Gabriel foothills
I'm still in a car at that point and the shape with its stiff—no—sturdy—no—strong lined like how dancers hold their leg lines—horizontal stretch. In my mind (there again) the wings are paddles pulled and then glide, pull and then glide—The great blue heron, high in its flight. I didn't know

[16] Pigeons all along. I find the tumblr post #lovepigeonsagain2016

In the meantime, hummingbirds are back some. And one morning I'm up for the bamboo birds to be overwhelming the ears. I'm up in time for them to raucous, for them to cacophony. That's a different marine layer day

Also all the corvids are traveling with mouthfuls—beakfulls—again

This morning, two big house finches
or a pair of small young parrots,
strung on wire

Last night, Sunday, with my Theandrew friends, we walk back under a sky that is a seagull migration.

This afternoon, or right before noon before 100 degrees, there's a pigeon paloma nest that wasn't there before, in one of the plane trees in the field where the students play and the sycamores are for the cooper's hawk in spring and the hummingbirds all year

And how here I am, the interstice | before that one writes me back | is still the time and place I write quickly and thoroughly

Maybe it <u>was</u> the moon but by now I don't think so, we've waned past

How Rocío is writing and how I am feel far apart today, but Wednesday when we were at her house I asked for copal and she lit the charcoal and I felt. Things felt. Aye and when I read what she wrote and she read what I wrote and it slipped back, turned in place, we're writing a book. Or something, but I hope a book.

This morning I was greeted so many times by my 8 to 10 year olds especially, and I had so many to greet. Greeting, like touching. (Sometimes together sometimes apart.) And touching, like greeting.

Each time I climb down from my house I walk in the street and there are so many people I don't greet. All year so far I know [to] how to write about each other, humans in bodies, but I'm badly present with my sleeping neighbors in our street, street we have in common, and so much none / more / ? This failing goes on and on behind this writing and I push it away again. Fuck.

Fall ends up starting with flying palomas, after I learn more of their history with us. It's that they are full beautiful in the park where I transfer between bus and train in Pasadena. It's green and there are plants and space. They do their loose flock swirls, wave motions, and all of their wings are grey on top and light under. I wait long enough for them to have a sound, and for them to cross between me and the sun and show that their translucence is almost there. Turning away towards my path it strikes me that the Holy Ghost Spirit lands in the form of a dove; that the holy ghost means paloma; that we collectively dismiss the pigeons in front of our faces; redacted

Last days summer—crow light shine shines sun back off into the eye bright sun of the beholder dark shine
which doesn't reflect light in the same way which reflects light in a different way—
bruise all over my body from—
the sound, finally, of raven flight, when I can see across their wing, back, and wing
the noise is not the wings beating against the air
the sound is the long strong (stiff) (rigid) feathers sliding over and across one another as the (meat) muscles pull and push (contract) into flying; the pinions and pinions; the pinions and (front / back   strong / speed   feathers) the pinions and the back body feathers<-

[24] I left the house once, at 7:30 p.m., and went on the roof, and read, and went in the pool after it got dark and cold, and now I've made tea in an effort to do things that can be everyday everyday

Before that, when I first came out on the roof, I was thinking how Murphy knew as soon as or before I did, and so had Jill, known, in a way; and maybe Katie, and Taylor asked even though I can't remember the words, and yeah

THOSE birds though. The ones that live in the bamboo—they were doing the wheel and float, turn and sail, wave and flock. The light was gorgeous. Like the young girl who lives in the other building called them, there's a red glow lit quickly on their wings in that light. They finally swoop dove into the canopy we have, the bamboo thicket, and settled themselves. Sudden urge to be in a row under the canopy, a WilSkills ridgeline.

"Hate of pigeons didn't start until the 20th Century. Before that was about 9,900 years of loving them..." "Pigeons live with us in cities because...we made them..." "I just have a lot of feelings about how complex and multidimensional pigeon hating is." @crisscrosscutout, OP, on tumblr #LovePigeonsAgain2016

OMFG and did I write you about seeing a goshawk fly though the Forest of Dean on TV?

[25] On the way, the hawk with the moves I can't describe to Rocío on text because I need my whole body to do it.
[here there is a drawing/diagram/sketch]
I can, in water, roll and glide with this kind of pull from span to body close stream line hull of my neck back shoulder
It's impossible for seraphim-angels-wingèd messengers—

[27] Yeah I said
yeah I said it babe

Animals no,
parrots, their thin
spread and few tail feathers
—green

Train, bus, mammal human configurations, yes

Machine technologies
flights lining up in the eastern string
to pass into LAX, yes
—way out past

"Michael deliver that baby
deliver that baby Michael!"
"Ew it looks like tortillas!"
(the internet on stingray births)

The heat breaks

I keep taking the bus and the train

The men and women sleeping on the street, I recognize
and more often than not in a position I sleep in
or a person I've loved does, or you do

On your side, arm curled under your head, head which rests in the crook of your elbow
knees drawn up, your other hand wedged between your knees for warmth or for the support it
gives your lower back or just to hold
yourself in place

Travesty is a position

The heat breaks

I leave my cool dark room and go up to the roof some evenings
The sun sets behind me
The light makes its change
The planes begin to line up for their evening landings
When I watch them come in I think of their father
The birds—not pigeons—not certain but maybe between starling and sparrow I'll figure it out—
murmurate
In groups which absorb, divide, separate, come back together, and repeat, in different numbers
each time, every third rushing sweep
They cut sharply over my head a few times
They land for the night in the bamboo thicket
The noise they make there and the noise sound their wings make with air
—real movement

Where is my person becomes: Who and how do I need to be for them to come? What arrangements
should I be making; I mean what can I do can I know to make them stay

September

how long do hummingbirds live?
the same visitation

[datura]

the ravens have their mouths full again

[datura]

change of air change in air
raven wing in air, the hard lilies family

more at dusk
raven matte black on one face of their wings
gold bright reflecting from the other face

[datura]

you're a child now
you're a child right now

[dátura dátura dátura]

because blue heron
great gray in the morning headed due west,
west-southwest, marine layer up around San Gabriel

strong lined how dancers hold
wings are paddles pulled and glide
pull and glide
I didn't know

[datura]

pigeons all along
hummingbirds
and one morning the bamboo birds
raucous, cacophony, a different marine layer

all corvids all traveling with beakfuls again
back under sky

[datura]

how unrelated I've come with water many times over
it was the moon
we've waned

[datura]

copal slipped back
turned in place
greeting, like touching and touching, like greeting

[dátura dátura dátura]

walk in the street all year
about each other's human bodies
sleeping neighbors
the street we have in common

[datura]

flying palomas with us
where it's green and plants and space

loose flock swirls
wave motions grey on top and light under
holy holy holy ghost ghost ghost
spirit

[datura]

the next days, last days summer
crow light shine
shines sun back into the eye
bright sun and dark sun
crow light reflects light a different way

[datura]

dark and cold
you wanted to see
you wanted to hear
gorgeous
(something adorning the throat)

[dátura dátura dátura]

the wheel and float
turn and sail
wave and flock
light gorgeous
the young girl called them and a red glow lit quickly on their wings

swoop dive into the canopy we do have
bamboo thicket urge to be in a row
to scatter shelter around a fire
to settle into canopy we do and do not have here

[datura]

on the tv in England, goshawks fly through canopy
in California, the hawk with the moves I can't describe because
I need my whole body in water
to roll and glide this pull from span to body
close stream line hull of neck back shoulder

[datura]

five pages of notes on investigative journalism
the heat breaks

my neighbors sleeping on the street and more often than not
sleep in a position I sleep in or you do

a person in this position must
if I were in your position I'd

[datura]

the heat breaks cool dark some evenings
light makes its change
planes line up for their evening landings
watch for them to come in

[dátura dátura dátura]

the bamboo thicket birds group, absorb, separate
come back together and repeat every third rushing sweep
cut sharply

land for the night
the noise they make there and sound their wings make with air together
real movement

[datura]

person becomes
who and how
I need
to be for them
to be for them to come
arrangements and derrangements
what can I do to make them
to make them
to stay

and the datura, the datura

positions and the Datura

[September]

You go to the sea, to the smell of the sea and the grasses. Always the sulfur smell, the bright patch of grass and crows over the aluminum buildings shouting at the cooper's hawk.
First days of school. You remember them, their bright eyes are tired now. B is still sick. He first got sick in your class all those years ago.

And then you are sick too, wrung out like a dish towel. For hours you sweat and weep on the floor. Ana is away, Denise too heavy a sleeper. You crawl back and forth the bathroom and think good thing kitten isn't here so I don't have to change the sheets till the morning.

Denise made a joke when the vomiting started: maybe you had done it/maybe this was it. First you want pregnancy at all costs/you became terrified of the costs.

Tuesday: it feels early, it feels late/ a white sliver of cliché just beyond the crescent leaves of the peach/ an alabaster beast long on the stone path.

A fruit fly in the whiskey.

Is a crow/corvidae/ a punished bird?

The ravens come/ receive their song of life happening. The good news is the gray morning. But then there is the letter, the phone call. You were okay, you learn to be okay each time but this time is hard. Your arms just became accustomed to his weight, his eyes just learned to find your eyes. How foliage drops, how it lifts in a stray breeze in front of your car. The canopy of Chinese elms on Linda Vista. The hand of the sky.

You are late to your teaching job because your face shows you are human. You are waiting in your car overlooking the rose bowl.

You remember how lent ends. You pick gravel from your knees and elbows and go home.
There's no place quite like here/there's no better time than now/that's why I stay ready.
(Your tooth is bleeding for no reason)

Fortnight. Water on the wilderness/ saplings coming along. The little ones out front had a rough summer. Just hang on, little. The spring will make you so big and strong. *Mother's neglect/ what brings the autumn*

*

An ankle (my ankle)

The calico finds you napping. You stay longer to be a pillow for her little neck/ your ankle pulsing.

Bougainvillea in echo park. Make a left at the lotus nursery. And later, the paraiso's yellow flower.

See her smile. Bear the thought of her body against her body, her fine bones and easy smile. And then see Jen, her tired smile, her arms without him. You feel needles inside your elbows.
Her long warm hug is for you more than for her. We say Paul's name.

Later, in the far corner booth under string lights, everyone laughing. Ana's sleepy look. Near the flag/ flag adjacent. You write how you were made and brought.

The bougainvillea on the porch. Her long arms reaching for the front door. I want to be where she opens her mouth.

Blood arrives on Thursday, the ache that comes from turning away, so we walk to filled places, to dark rooms and spilled drinks, to the roar of crowds, a whole pack of us, moving from bar to bar in the city of yucatecos on the boulevard of no Alamos. The weight of us, of you.

A love letter to us all/ the table you can't have sex on/ light light

You walked ahead of the boys, she laughed and it made you happy.

*

(I saw the mangled butterfly)

Frank Ocean/ cry in the shower/what it is to do that in a time of drought/ I'd do anything for you (in the dark)

I saw K today- she is safe but her lip trembles a little and her eyes shift.

An equinox and what has changed

The sea air, mother and father in the desert/ the first time driving that way/my father telling me what the salton sea was/ the palo verde, the álamo and chamizos and the all american canal (a student asks why that line in Spanish/ the poet answers: the line demanded it)

Late now: so hung over. out with the cats/ the phrase demands from you. Face your students wearing your glasses. Wash your hands in the green light. You pronounce their language correctly and they are proud of you. you are happy to make them proud.

you can't tell her (but I'm telling you) how the calico held the dovelet in her mouth how she was so broken her eyes wide open her chest heaving her neck broken so you held her underwater until she stopped struggling which wasn't long and then you buried her under the peach tree and the geranium.

You went west but not to the sea, though you can smell it. Gather basil. Rub it on your arms/ eat it. Little sparrow, watched. Lemons gathered washed and sorted. Somewhere a season wants to turn/ but turn to what.

(You said to me can I tell you/I said yes/you said to me/ I don't know if I want to ask/ that's I wanted to tell you)

Aliso

Where hanging bodies turn sepia courtyards spring up
around you shades flutter open from dreams of floods
deliver, misnamed, the butcher's block,
the arms for lovers to swing from
cling to riverbanks, that bone that juts from the pelvis,
the clavicle a nest of corvids –
is that the call that springs/
from your throat that calls for return/
again, rain, again or fire or flame—
(how tawny and mottled your leaves
curling from thirst)
sore from shouting your voice the song of
lovers sighing in the barren valley
you learned the names of the others
they're tongues not of people, they called you sycamore.

A Yellow Flower Falling

Bear the thought of a body
against a body/the fine tissue
the nest that wilts in rainfall—
the house that wants to be haunted—

or arms ringing empty
as bells (except at least) a bell
has that thing/
(cages) our bodies
for a little bird we might trap
or for ourselves when enough time has gone by/
we toast and laugh even without children
(even as radiation approaches).
We don't imagine the finches eating poison
under the chinaberry tree
from which that yellow flower fell.

Bougainvillea

Ornament being the devil you bloom under that body
long arms reach for doors/what use are locks
when the key is in the tongue/or below it
thorny boughs/ *thicket* she said/
come briars through that window
find the fine wrists, the finger pointing to sleep
let us pave the way to hell with other people
this phrase or that in which language and for what
so that we can be there, where mouths open.

[October] all of the week of Hurricane M I write nothing but texts with my sisters and mother.

the hurricane passes

All week crows and ravens, parrots, little birds, and pigeons. No hawks.
Two vultures—first time since July going north on the train. Their wings, the two tones of brown and browngrey, opaque and translucent.
On instagram I start looking at the Audubon photos every day.
Hummingbirds and hawks. Repeat.

But I feel a bat, my colony is several thousand miles away in Portugal, in the palace of Mafra library. Going through the windows at night to the orchards and flowers, coming back for the insects who eat at the book papers and glues, nocturnal. Spending the day still and downside up behind the cases.

I speak with Moa on the phone. She asks can she use part of our letter I wrote her for a film, a new one she's working on.

Redacted—the first night—and I'm angry with my skin heating and my reticence inflamed with resentment. In the night I dream I have my chest covered, completed redacted anger that comes out there instead of my grinding mouth and tensed throat. When I look in the mirror they are all different sizes, and I'm supposed to meet someone and I am already so uncomfortable with my body—
It turns out to be a dream, but the kind where I'm surprised the next morning in the mirror that the blemishes feel sitting there aren't visible.

At the dinner Sam invites us to, I look at her a lot. Her young-oldness is stark. My lack of partner isn't noticed by anyone but me—this isn't Bridget Jones or something—no one is trying to set me up. Does anyone know that I want, that I began to notice how bereft it makes me and now I notice all the time?

After the reading and long book event day, Jen and Rocío gather succulents. Succulenters gonna suc-culent. Stop. Go to sleep. You've been dreaming, of late. Of sleep. And waking. I see the high schooler on the Altadena bus again, the one with Theandrew's face shape and bones. Sleep. Go. Yesterday someone on the roof had his kind of laugh. I could hear it from outside my room. Go to bed.

[7] strange street harassment

[12] the datura reappears, three blooms on the smallest plant, two open. In noon high warmth. How.

[13] For the third time, the young man—the Theandrew one with his jaw, his skull, his timbre of skin, but taller—boards the bus and rides and debarks.

For the umpteenth time, motorcycles. For the near umpteenth time, one that chooses the lane between me in a van going 70 or 80 and the next lane and its speeding vehicle. For the near umpteenth time, a motorcycle mirages behind in the rearview mirror, then mirages out of sight, then back into sight, still behind me. What umpteenth must mean is: that one no longer expects it to stop, though the feeling of it always affects in the same way, even when you anticipate it. I ask my sisters about animals where they are. In Oregon Jude is laughing and has begun to crawl. In delight to finally move, I imagine.

[13] under the raven's wing right at sun up—layered dispersing—the light hits it gold and rose gold. Later in the SCI-Arc bookstore there are sheets in packages, and a kind of kit, for gold leaf and silver leaf to gild with.

walk by the Harry Dodge & Octavia Butler shows at Armory each day after work too

Walking home (on Ninth, easterly) ran into Chiwan's mom and dad. We hugged in the middle of the crosswalk and his mom held my hand until we parted.

[14] corvid with nothing in their mouth the way they land—my language supplies a mechanical description—landing gear and the plane leaning back nose up

[15] fucked redacted or rather what Nicole and Lisa and I call redacted. I take the bus home down Seventh and it's broad Saturday daylight. It feels good to be home alone all day waiting out the hangover. Hooking up—this year has been the year of getting myself off—feels rare and out of character but in no way shameful. I note myself wishing for cuddling—is that the right word? bodies holding each other together quietly—and maybe some syrup slow sex—but meh hooking up. It's an itch and it goes away.

[16] the birds *and* how flight isn't dancing it's more a combination of (some kind of really fight / aggressive / intense metaphor) and synchronized swimming but like, warp speed and cut throat Black Swan

[24] ravens tandem flying can't resist emotion sensation
hawk I see and show Danielle she sees everything before me
Rain making the mountains taller, their "massif" quality—broadness swelling at their bases
And: Big thunder after everywhere lightning
the bamboo thicket birds: *every sundown attend / and it began to rain*

[25] dátura dátura dátura (blackberry...) Da tu ra Da tu ra Da tu ra—straw furls in shade overnight more overnight deep green and dust resistant
pink dove talk to get pigeon noises trees stumps—which page of *The Giving Tree*—and I fucking hate that book
hummingbird chatters at the entrances
the wind after the rain the moon crescenta almost finished waning

some of these dreams man. It's "owloween" on the Audubon Society

Can you even remember?

[26—27] I finally turned off my intuition about (towards) redact. Eased off? Withdrew? (Severed, cut off.) It's leaving lots of time on my hands. To like, read? I still have it, in the times before and after we see each other in person. Way less though—before, I could smell them on the weather. Scent them, really: Like coyote, wolf, hound, bear, horse, deer, jackrabbit, panther-mountain lion-cougar-puma-painter, and as them.

yeah but no you're still writing about this, exercising / exorcising

[28] *Mysterious Fires* (Harry Dodge, 2016) is a single channel video, color, sound; 24m30s. I see it at the Armory. I recommend it very much. From the promotional imagery for the show, a still taken from this piece, I assumed it would be weird in a grating or aggressive way. It was weird, I guess, in the way playfulness is weird—in the way nerding out on big ideas / freaking out is weird—in the way very smart people are weird. I laughed more than once aloud.

I don't know if it's the memory of *The Argonauts* first scene under my mind while I see Harry Dodge's body in the videos—moving through the world and gestures or these sentences copied out on the board but I wrote You can do anything you want to me as long as we do it slowly first and got, felt, wet.
The light changed when I exited the building in the way it does for

[30] days hath October and one more;
cricket;
cricket;
and angry, walking around and feeling in me anger. Chestplayed, flush blooming from below my skin
do you think I'm getting in touch with anger / sensation / emotion thereof out of my rear view? Yes.
Do you think it's something to do with all this fic you've been reading? Fic includes rainbows of emotion including all these angers from many different characters. *Role modeling*!!!
Recognition / identification / _____ (the word that means these somatically including non-brain organs!) / parasympathetic mirroring?

[30 and 31] and there is was, the end of this month, an actual autumn feeling in my air. The thing of it is, only on the roof do I feel out of doors, and not exactly even then. Altadena in the morning is a sight to see—smell feel on the skin. It's not outside-out though.
I got there too late for the flying but in time for the cacophonying

[31] and all the birds; the kiddos. Getting twitchy, some of them. Meeting with no one in the afternoon. Happy there. And on the roof, got the flying. My gorgeous. Light slantwise across them, their banking air sail waves, magic: lightness of being? (From *able*, from *power*.) Fleet-ness of being

As if you were, so be

Feel bat
Make still days

Feel vulture
Opaque the sky

Feel anger
Stake skin

Feel insect
Shake pollen

Feel hurricane
Ache on past

Feel *them*
Wake there

Feel datura
Break timbre green

Feel raven
Quake light

Feel motorcycle
Mistake

Feel dream
Lake under

Feel coyote
Take scent

Feel painter
Forsake canopy

Feel hummingbird
Flake gossamer

Feel want
Snake up true

Feel child
Rake fast water

Feel paloma
Slake purple

Feel moon
Mandrake

Feel bat
Feel bat

Sense-feeling

Feel a bat making still days a vulture opaque the sky an anger stake skin an insect shaking pollen a hurricane ache on past Feel *them*, wake there Feel datura break timbre green a raven quake light a motorcycle mistaking Feel a dream lake under a coyote take scent a painter forsake canopy a hummingbird flake gossamer a want snaking up true a child raking water a paloma slake purple Feel the moon mandraking
Feel a bat feeling a bat

after The Inner Reality of Ultra-Intelligent Life—Harry Dodge at the Armory

You can do anything you want with me as long as you do it slowly first
You can do anything you want to me as long as you do it slowly
You can do anything you want with me to me
We can do anything you want as long as you do it slowly
We can do anything as long as we do it slowly first
We can do anything
I'll do anything you want with you as long as we do it slowly first
I'll do anything you want to you as long as we do it slowly first
We can do anything we want to me
We can do anything we want to you
We can do anything we want to us as long as we do it slowly first
You can do anything you want with us as long as you do it slowly first
You can do anything you want to me as long as we do it slowly first

[October]

You said to me can I tell you/I said yes/you said to me/ I don't know if I want to ask/ that's I wanted to tell you

*

the new moon comes black and a twin. The other will come late, the way my sister and I were born. Saturday is difficult. The fox is in tears/ she is tired. We set up the record player and she is happy.

Carnell Snell is killed at 107th St. A mother has to beg uniformed strangers past the plastic tape (and their guns) to put her hands on the body of her boy.

and then a new year, the day the world began, even as the wilderness wilts. Leaves fall. Things are better in the morning.

On your mother's porch. The sansevieria, how swords reach for the moth's death. the dead hydrangea, dusty pink corymb- how a flower drinks acid and blooms. Mother gives you an amaryllis bulb. *She had a friend named Amaryllis who lived on Carmelita and Randolph. You perched on your heels in front of the snowy screen while the mothers chatted. Her youngest son Freddy was a terror at school and shorter than you, but angry. Her oldest son was in a bed and couldn't speak.*

How long, hummingbird? The annunciation / visitation different only by feather

The datura/datura/ that sleep time

The nightshade's perfect berry

Dark and cold (you wanted to see)

something adorning the throat

what we do/ and do not have (arrangements)

she holds the mandarin peel like a flower

The dancers' line: flamenco

(I didn't know)

mouthful

beakful

the one-hundred degrees days

*

I think my favorite month of the year is February

*

how a year is new now. Drive to Claremont. Steal succulents in a parking lot: blue curl echeveria, kalanchoe tetraphylla, fire stick. We sit in a college town pub and you get that young feeling. You argue with Rachel about a gardenia and you look it up. You are right but you don't show it to her.

an anniversary. The river reed and the pearl of occident at their desert marriage. How often can I write about the orange blossom and the whiteness of her.

eyeliner

(the eyeliner)

a tuesday night café: at the Far Bar by myself and then finding my wolf pack and then sitting at a long table singing eternal flame. Someone says Pretty Good For A Bunch Of Writers. We laugh a good laugh. It feels good to laugh.

Every 7th: detonate: the wilderness in an exposed photograph, radiografía se dice

on a different page (she and I)/there is that kind of carnage

Friday: A neon museum/ noir.

Saturday: Megan's birthday.

Watch this televised talk in horror. (I write about being the grabbed person)

*

the death of the reef. little bone, little hand waving goodbye. The ornament, that is.

*

what you wait for when it is the only thing to wait for/ that

Monterey Park hospital. Here the place of your birth. The syllables you learned in English at age four.

The floors smell clean but not antiseptic. Your father smiles cheerfully. You learn something you didn't know. *something about clean hands.* You have a feeling he has never lied to you, not even to protect your feelings. You are afraid, you have not returned the favor. *what if not blood.*

(the train together. I usually take the train alone. I talk to a guy who has his head against his hands.)

We walk down to broadway and 9th and drink ginger and lemon tea and talk wirecutter business.

And after, there is guacamole and chips and I finish the bottle of whiskey and she doesn't drink any more.

Columbus Day October 12th. After the cockfight there is soft down and congealed blood and scratches on the dirt from where we tried to stand our ground. The tail feathers were confiscated.

Chilaquiles and the rain out on the porch with tea and coffee. The trees the steady mist green hummingbird, two fussy corvids. Scout prancing.

Halloween: the lights outside the window in the hedges

The bougainvillea leaves gathered on the porch.

Desert

What telling is

> Is here/here is a map/is a line
> greetings from this green place. I miss your thirst
> your turning in the dark your always tired and always sad
> your days are only okay your nights long and restless
> your always broken body your always somewhere below your body
> absent from my body/that wild place
> /
> *how long, hummingbird?* The annunciation / visitation different only by feather
> the line in the sand the citrus peels in her hand or what is my hands was it me
> who crushed the leaves to hold to your face I forget
> (what hands forget) they made too much coffee they forgot they wouldn't
> carry a cup to you

Night/shade

One the long sleep /the other the mercy of the children you are starving.
At night lit up the wilderness allows this
allows your boots and three times filled glass to stand
under the still-green peach in hopes of rain: *what we can muster*.
(in this dry place)
the datura/dátura/ that sleep time.
Dark and cold (you wanted to see)
something adorning the throat
what we do/ and do not have (arrangements)

The Dreaming

Someone had to dream this/us/ a sun covered in necklaces
we met once where mouths were mute:
before time, in the dark land, a navel, a tower of Babel
sing to life a son
(if that's all it took I'd still be childless)
I saved words from the storm to sew into my body
there (you are) a map the way back home:
a strange dark face in the mirror/mine.

On the Death of the Reef

Little bone, little hand waving goodbye. The ornament, that is.
What you wait for when it is the only thing to wait for/ that
(the habit of raising stolen things)
you grow them in lieu of a reef
the ripple and flourish of waves, of membrane thickening/hardening
how a year is new now. Drive to Claremont.
blue curl echeveria, kalanchoe tetraphylla, fire stick.
Mandarin/
she holds the mandarin peel like a flower
mouthful/beakful
those one-hundred degrees days
We sit in a college town pub and you get that young feeling.
Young enough to laugh and ovulate at the thought.

Friday: neon noir

How light is contained how

the dark face in the mirror/mine

darkness is harnessed how thunder how prayer
how words are uttered in supplication: *please.*

Cloistered as pearls/clutched as eggs
(what is it they say about hell and high water?)
outside the mysteries of/
what does fact matter
when there is truth there is your hand
on my neck there is the memory of breath
and bare shoulders
(you think of the sea/that kind of carnage/
a roaring shell empty and pretty as mouths)
and eyeliner.

[1 November] All Saints with Rocío. Up too early, passing by too early, for the cacophony these days; will it change with the Pacific Daylight Time returning to Pacific Standard Time? Monice's book, and our attendance office hours, and quesadillas (*the* answer to the snax feeling), and we meet Jessica at Sonny's. She's good. There's going to be a baby. We feel. I love her.

[2] All Souls; Día de los Muertos. The birds for almost half an hour. A word that is spellbound but not. Spell*un*bound. An unbounding spell. One sense of self is ~~thought~~ felt to have come from Old English (or Old High German?) "spilian," "to play;" ah. Swells of play. You know, charm is also from chanting. Bind—to make captive or also a swaddling sense in there somewhere (and perhaps still, bdsm?) To stick together. But also, bend, from the same Proto-Indo-European *bhendh, with join-strive-strain-bend, and, partner. A bending or curving. The skater Julie Kindstrand (Jules Lynn), she does the gorgeous lines in pools, those empty oblong weird curved pools.

[3] I'm walking up to roof Right Now for birds. Nicole and I will meet folks at Venice Room. Togetherness rituals and a change of mind about "alone together," but I can't remember what my mind has changed to.

[4] Don't remember except evening bamboo thicket birds. Someone else was up here so I was, had to share the space. The smog, the air pollution haze in the air, catches and holds the light at the end of the day in a way that's muddy, thick heavy colors. Now when I see it I think about Katie and that conversation in Seattle down by her trapeze rig in Georgetown. And some pigeons skim me, underwings white.

[5] lots of time on the metro, isn't it? People-people. Not in a way of "more / realer" or "authentic angelenos!" though I acknowledge I have felt those things. In a way of: There and there and here and over there and over here are people, I know not only because of seeing hearing and smelling; there is that other way which is more to do with vibration in air, with taking up a certain amount of space, with the espalda sensation of presence, entity.

I go with Meg and the Bobs to see The Eagle Huntress on Santa Monica Boulevard...) and !!!!!!! It is beautiful. The usual documentary questions are there but!!!! Crying. Plus of course this depiction of a father and a child, a daughter.

The middle of November is the birds, of course, sometimes in much smaller enumerations (annunciations) and sometimes coming to home in scores at a time instead of the hundred, hundreds, at once. The savings time has ended so I come home from work, fiddle around, and go up to the roof about 4:30 p.m. Lately I see two neighbors, a couple, we've watched together three times, me bursting to tell them what the grand finale will be and barely resisting. And with my neighbor Jessica, Jess, several times now. I suspect she goes up like I used to, not for the birds but to call home (that'll be Greenwich Mean Time, seven hours off our Pacific Standard) and at times just breathe under sky.

The election disarrays us all. The pigeons, ravens, squirrels, human creatures in front of me, blur. The roof bird visits are all that make sense. If before was or wasn't these feelings about human flocks, human homecomings, daily human together-and-apartness, movement, communication—now these are overwhelming each dusk. Bird o'clock.

[10] The arrays and severings on social media are one place I look—the protest I go to with Jessica, Doug, and Claire is another. The drumming and chanting at the middle feels stagnating,

dominating, even as it calls to the urge within me for order, for direction, for accomplishment; for, horribly, corporate "action items" speech.

The drums, chants, groups, further from that center feel different in purpose—connected to and responding around the speakers—but at any time risking diffusion, wandering, drifting. Stay together!!! I feel. Spread out!!! I feel. Make decisions in a great field of awareness beginning with those nearest you—It's keen, in a protest in a wide street, a long ribbon of distance from front to back. Do we have great fields of sensing, flocks attracting one another, landing in a great flourish—or other dusks never quite grouping altogether, flocking in one small grouping at a time—but still all into the thicket.

And no silent rest in either case. Long loud hours of bird noise, moving around, taking more time to rearrange there than to spinwheel the shimmered formation. Noisy joyful, noisy angry, noisy putting each other in places, noisy claiming, noisy calling out to find friends and roost-mates. Do they end up in a different sleep perch each night? HOURS of this. Near dawn when they wake up it's less goodnight goodnight and more good morning GOOD MORNING and wake up! and hello! hello and day! and chatter plans. Possibly for diabolical and liberating actions; chattering nonetheless.

This is all imaginations, the only imagination of joy and movement in the full week. Everything else is hundreds of words of walls from me and to me. My sisters we're all having familiar trauma responses and it doesn't change it enough to recognize. We see it in everyone we know who has lived in extended familial abuse

I take it back—there was joy being with Jessica that night—there was joy being in solidarity with my sisters—there was comfort in greeting the kiddos at school—there was laughter and hopefulness in Teka's writing—there was wry togetherness in dry, dry humour.

None of this feels *new*, only *acute*, only overt to some people who wouldn't hear the whistles before. (Not couldn't. Not this time.)

[14] I finally go see the moon, hiding out from light all weekend, and see Jess. With her the right word for the birds: Mesmerizing. (And in a French accent the voiced consonants between the vowels vibrate in the exact right way.) I'd forgotten how it is to talk U.S. politics with a French national my age. Naïma and Eva I remember talking 2005 about U.S. going into fucking war in Iraq. (That syntax still telling: war <u>in</u> Iraq, war <u>in</u> Afghanistan, war <u>in</u> Yemen, war <u>in</u> Syria, war <u>in</u> Libya, war <u>in</u> Nigeria, war <u>in</u> Pakistan. Never "with" never "against." Lands to be fought over, not sovereignties to be reckoned with.) "A thousand years of ties to that [*literal*] soil," Jess says. Her father's side of the family meeting her mother's side in an ongoing imperial riptide.

The point is, the (so useful) blinding idealism just isn't there on the continent, and when it is it's identified with the supremacist white right. Here in the U.S. the "left" politicians still elect themselves with this obligatory rhetoric and seem to believe is themselves. Or at least they make a much better job of acting it than any centrist European I can think of. The point is, Jess is living in a slow burn and from where she sits it's moving in the good direction, only it cannot be hurried. I had forgotten what it was like to wish I saw the world this way. I can't and I don't; still it was a bath of an encounter with another perspective.

It made me long to spend time with my Jessica, soak in her eyes more. There was more, there was, but an animal drought—now meaning I'm not doing the visiting.

[16] the woman on the train behind me is making strange noises. Her bird wants something to eat. It isn't inside the paper grocery bag—it's on her shoulder eating cracked seed. "What kind of bird is it?" (He? They?) "A pineapple-headed grinchy con-er parrot." Repeat, word for word. "That's right, most people don't get it all at the first time." Gray yellow, bright yellow, warm blue, red orange. As tall as my hand. She's talking to the bird just sitting here on the train. Imagine your life with a bird on your shoulder, walking up and down to your forearm. "Most parrots don't start talking until they're about two you know." I don't, I don't know anything, I want to know how it got to her (pet store downtown, which means by my street) and how it got to there (afraid to ask). In passing she mentions all the other birds she's had who've died on her or sickened or escaped. She learned her lesson: No more thinking up perfect names. "This one's Pineapple and anyway that's what she was used to being called. It only took her a day, by the end of our first day she knew her name." I'm dying to take a picture of them together, this white woman probably 60, 65 years old, and her fair hair, no makeup except bright blue color in a thick line on her upper eyelid. I can't tell anything else about her. She gets off at Chinatown. Later it turns out she was saying Pineapple-headed Green Cheek Conure Parrot, and I'd changed the bird's green into blue because of the thick line of color on her eyelids.

[17] getting on the train to see Rocío and as it pulls through Union Station, two pigeon palomas on the arms of a man, still life, then motion: a couple more on the ground, him sitting on a bench, the cup of his hand with cracked corn in the palm. *A hand that remains / open*

[18] Rocío's cats. Lady literally falling of her bench over my leg. The birds! this time again, the flocking questions: Two pigeons join, or try, not quite built for the bobsled freeform / air slalom of the murmurers; their wings too long & more suited to diving glides, their bodies' meat muscles, long-twitch fibers, lag in response to the cuts and banking wind turn of the bamboo birds fast-twitch muscles. They are there, though, and disappear / reappear in the matrix, ever-volving cascade of rain sheets.

I'm put in mind of Bascom Lamar Lunsford's recording of Swing Low, which he learned from a black preacher in North Carolina between 1900 and 1950. (He did not say the man's name when he recorded this version at the Smithsonian.) *Swiiingg—all around me—swing low, chariot, swing low.* It's a quick rhythm version, the picked-out banjo notes are quick underneath it too.

[19] helicopters still going when I feel asleep last night; helicopters starting when I'm still waking up this morning. About an hour later no helicopter sound. But as soon as I write this I hear it return from the other side.

[21] I left unsettled. All this time I'd felt clearly the hopeful possibilities of their gorgeous (throat-catching again) flights, matrices of organized moving? and not the gut wrenching hydra-capacity for evil this shapeshifting presents. To pose and fight a shapeshifting hydra surely requires a shapeshifting collective determined to bring all of themselves home to roost.

[22] Rocío got here right at bird o'clock and we watched until the flock roosted. It didn't feel over and it wasn't. (It had seemed like some of them were already in in the canopy.) They flew down and off in small groups, until all of them were above and aloft. It was gorgeous, throat catching. (Oh yes and Rocío saw, before twilight, the birds high-high seeming to gather loosely or survey or prepare.) Then there was a hawk, low and headed loosely down Maple towards the yucatecos around the park on the corner of Fifth and San Julian or maybe Sixth and Gladys.

Finally! Rocío and I wait and quiet, sync, the birds land all together this time. Silent still bamboo whooshes into bedtime, the ordered chaos. Then! Hawk? Swoops across the top of the bamboo canopy and pulls up at the last minute, lands on a ledge perpendicular to us. Hawk, "look," I say. "Peregrine falcon," Rocío breathes. The slimness of the tail feathers and their length, balancing the perch; the shortness of the neck and shape of the head; she must be right. Later I look in *Birds of North America*. And *le cri*. "Flight is fast; rarely soars. Preys almost entirely on birds. Call is a long series of slurred notes." Falco Peregrinus.

[23] last night we attended the birds at bird o'clock, the bird hour, I think like witching or magical light, this way of speaking, and. We ate quesadilla, queso fresco on corn tortilla, tomato, avocado from Eva's house. *From here* foods. And read each other poems, short and weird, weird and I asked how to make my poem doing what it does for me to translate. And her poems, that first one, is naked as fuck, naked as the day it was born.

I also narrowed down and the bamboo birds are for certain: EUROPEAN STARLING. Sturnus vulgaris.

"Told from true blackbirds by its short tail and, in flight, by its browner wings. Spends the night in large communal roosts from late summer until spring. Often an abundant pest in city parks, suburbs, and farms. Song is largely of squeaky notes, but it imitates many bird calls."

"Starlings (Family: Sturnidae), introduced and widespread in North America, are short-tailed, dark, and fat-bodied. Gregarious and aggressive, they are especially abundant at roosting sites. Diets are varied. Blue eggs (four to six) are laid in nest hole."

Now where the fuck are they laying their eggs? In that plot of soil under the bamboo and three palms?

Okay so I think the starlings stay in spring/summer plumage here? There's an illustration that includes a starling in flight. It's definitely them. *Hence.* We pestilent. We win the world by homing. Be reconfiguring constantly. By being *loud*. By adapting to many environments and diets, thriving everywhere. Hiding our blue fragile treasure. Aggressively assembling to prevent being picked off one by one. Rituals!! Flights!! Starlings are "perching birds," i.e., Order: Passeriformes. Three toes in front and one in back, longer. "Feet well-adapted for perching."

[24] Thanksgiving afternoon I'm down on the walk north of the pier. The gulls and terns seem like they're going on last long glides before bedding for their nights. There's huddling involved, I think. I'm spending the night watching The Fall, again, alone with Gillian Anderson.

Hannah texts the family thread to watch out for bears. (Like not to hit them in the dark road.) I think she must be on Town Mountain, at least, or Reem's Creek or Sweeten Creek or Fairview or near the balds. She describes what sounds like a juvenile, off-black, 250 pounds, crossing but sitting to the side of the road waiting for her car to drive by. They're smart this year she says, and there are so many in the city. Someone got a 500 pound one inside city limits. I think of the Sespe River, 30 miles north of Ventura, 15 miles from Ojai north on the 33, and that around the corner encounter with the big brown black bear. In retrospect I am surprised that bear even recognized me in the royal sense of, present oneself in court / speak with personhood status—honored. After that hike in the dark, unwilling to make camp until I put a few miles between us, I looked it up and yeah, black bears are only supposed to reach 500 pounds as an upper limit. Clearly not. To have such agility at such a size. Uphill, of course, better than down. Center of gravity reasons. Us, agility, moves, again.

[25] On the bus, or no, walking to the stop around 10:30 a.m. at Venice / Centinela a slow swirl, pigeons. Looking, catching my attention at first for the similarity to the starlings. They were first, though, remember at the beginning of the year, the balustrade? So making fun of the two pigeons trying out for the starling evening show wasn't correct.

Nona and I went to movies at Highland Park, then a drink next door. A good thing, to spur of the moment get together. A dog came after Winston and Nona saved him but I was so worried she put her hands in, so got bit. Barely broke skin but she's shaken, worried about Winston.

[26] stayed in with the rain. Dashed up to the roof for the birds (every day more adjectives, vivacious, garrulous, fierce) but they were settled under the canopy. I wonder how much of a shield that is. I was disappointed not to see Jessica (and felt funny / mad / sorry for myself that she and Rocío were spending that time together, not realizing any reasons, like for example, do you want harder what you can't have) and still feel some tenderness there. It passes. They're my people. A feel. Very lone wolf.

[27] came out only at bird o'clock, bird time, show time. Jess was up here, my second floor neighbor, and we greeted and watched and kept eyes and ears out in the world together. Both feeling to-our-selves.

Ah here they go: 4:44 p.m. Just a handful. It's cold up here, it is, and two neighbors I don't know are in the place I usually set myself out of the wind. These starlings, God. I love them. Amy just texted fifteen minutes ago, "Rach I'm pregnant again" ✳ ✳ ✳

[29] Crows, six, at the Figueroa and Lincoln stop (Altadena, bus 267). Playing the wind currents of the steep-roofed Seventh Day Adventist church. Across the way there's a palm stand so they land and repeat. Again thinking of a kayak in the eddies and waves of a section of river rapids, not so intense as Frank's Bells on the French Broad. Maybe more like the upper section of the Nantahala, or where the Cartecay's stretch of rapids is running high and fast with winter rain. Play boating, some people call it I think, when you put in at the rapids just to surf the waves there. I never went beyond a four (rating of a rapid) or so in a single open boat canoe. Never ran the Nolichucky. I like the Pigeon but never ran it in the winter. I know I'll never put in on the Green. Deaths every year that upper section.

The last three days are hawks again!! A big ole redtail spinning its way up to its height over the Hahamongna, biding its time from the lip of the bluff, barely seeming to gain altitude, steady in flight, but I take my eyes off for one minute, my attention caught by the big ravens calling loud to each other about it. The hawk and its pink backlit tail are high high, about twice the height of the drop into the watershed, and then in another blink too far to distinguish profile, shape, body. A dark ascending *what*?

The big guy (though, girl? who fattens like this?) who eats fat and happy where the "710" meets the 210 and Colorado, is perched and I swear I think first of a whale. Redtail, I guess, hawk profile but so so fat. They prey on rodents and small warm mammal bodies like this one I think. The last days November are many ravens and some crows. Rocío's and my talk, her with her dad, is there a way to tell crows and ravens apart in Spanish? To tell apart, to <u>say</u> apart. Differentiation and or description. Description with or without differentiation. The littlest ones. Their tails / tail's feathers.

Many times now I have known the sound of feathers under one another in the way of a fan. Not the accordion kind, the other kind with a structure like a deck of cards glued to popsicle sticks. There it is again, a comparison of the natural history to the technological one, in an effort to <u>tell</u>.

[30] November the birds, it's cold about 5 p.m. and filtered cool light glows without reflection. My neighbors, the couple, are already there; the one man offers to put out his j, but I'm like it's ok no worries. When they finally home / hone in, they dive rather than ascend. The other neighbor, the woman and I marvel *We've never seen them do that before!!* I thought of magnets, when you begin to attract iron filaments...a few more...a few more; then the pull of them seems to tip over and be irresistible. I wish to draw or animate, or really to gesture, or to live in a language which uses signs in space near and peripheral to my body, rather than producing vibrations in the space of the mouth to emit near my body.

The nightmare in night of the 29th and 30th, the nightmare was long and varied and began from good dreams. She wouldn't look at me. Is what I remembered and feel. She wouldn't look.

Nine Day Wonders (collocation)

Time in November is six crows landing and repeating.
Six crows at play above palms and churches; even their landings.

The starlings keep their time, gut wrenching.
Shapeshifting.
Hydra-tic ethics, helix.
I didn't see it / It appeared to me

The hawk and its pink back-lit tail spiral up.
They become a dark, ascending the air over.

Uphill, the bear recognizes me beneath her notice. *startle texture*
Big, brown-black bear, and walks away, and leaves me, alone.

Soon starlings will fill the soil with their blue eggs.
They are told from true blackbirds by their aggressions.
by their capacity for aggression.

romania quoque ab eodem prodigio novendiale sacrum publice susceptum est
sen voce caelesti ex albano monte missa—nam id quoque traditur—seu aruspicum monitu

Starling (v.)

The bamboo birds filter cool light.
They glow without reflection.

Gulls and terns glide long home.
The wind kicks up slow and strong.

She wouldn't look at me.
The nightmare was long and varied and began from good dreams.
She wouldn't look

tide (n.)

no more thinking up perfect attendance but work on the colors.
grey yellow, bright yellow, warm blue, red orange *red orange*

on a low swing, low swinging: pick out banjo notes and barely break them,
barely let when break skin, shake, shaken

rain cascade on the flock and the birds and her *!!!*
her word, *mesmerizing*, even disarrayed in this rough water

Haggard (adj.)

Prepare to gather loosely how to gather loosely.
Homing in flight, in winter plumage.
In not letting each another be picked off one by one.

A hawk, low and loosely towards the yucatecos.
Crying, gorgeous, *described as kree-eee-ar,*
her flight and her scream pitch high and slur downwards.
Formel, tiercel, eyasses, passager, haggards, redtail.

A falcon sharp-swoops the bamboo thicket:
Pull up silently and kill later, or pull up silently and miss the kill.
Rocío breathes peregrine
silhouette.

Time is fastslow. Time here and next door.
There hasn't been an other side.

Sooth (n.)

La resaca a current not a tide.
A current not a tide, a current not a tide
Array and sever, ribbon. *family choices in ongoing imperial riptide*

The rip means rupture in the water.
The delirium means off the furrow. *work stoppage*
The delirium crosses off the earth thrown up between two

Disarray blurs pigeons, ravens, squirrels, human creatures;
blurs stark daylight, blurs noise. To blur, to water down.

Visitation at the roof is movement at speed, is sooth-saying;
endless calibrating of time and place and relation.
restoring and *co-responding*
yet this *bringing back again*

to neighbor each other, watch three times
to come home to oneself needs neighboring
enumerations and annunciations

crying,
a certain amount of space
espalda sensation
a way of here and there and over there and over here, present

Twilight (adj.)

Dusk, a color-word originally;
pigeon palomas skim, underwings white-grey,
mud haze catches and holds the light at the end,
thickening the color.
Half-light appears twice a *day*
Togetherness rituals for birds. *Fff, that's for the birds*

Bind, swaddling; bend, play. Charm, chanting.
To partner, curve. Unbinding, wakeful, against hallucination,
the good kind of spell, made of breathing rather than taking away.

All Souls go off into the world later.
The new moon is up too early
is passing by too early.

[November]

You reread the claiming of sleeping beauty and sleep alone, wanting the kiss that doesn't wake you.

Somewhere there are waves. There is the sea.

The night of the thin veil you paint a room light pink in hopes of a place like that.

Coral reefs die, bleached as cotton. Bones waving under water.

What fear is when it grips you alone in broad daylight

Water- a little green here and there. The pineapple guava. The beasts on it.

A day for souls (what souls are/ are wreaths of smoke/are leaves that cling through winter) elms shudder in the lingering heat this is it, sighs the hillside. What names do (hold page of book)/ mark calendar.

Normally/normal/ you paint your face and venture out. This year you make a quiet offering to your guardians, the wilderness still with anticipation/ the hillside sighs with relief we are not forgotten the unlit candles the orange flowers on a Wednesday.

Marigolds- a name of a halo, of a lady.

How the tongue seeks the teeth, how lips push away, a short guttural vowel as if you are not expecting something (what were you expecting). And again teeth and breath and the tiny trill behind the tongue. How your people engineered speech, and song. How the growl of the jaguar and the chatter of the hummingbird. The sound of rain in your mouth, the slumber of volcanoes under snow.

Cempazúchitl/ instrucciones: romper la cabeza y regar los pétalos en forma de sendero o de cruz o del nombre del muerto. Asteraceae- en referencia a los astros. Estrellita en la mano, farolito en el frio.

Dejen las luces prendidas, que vengo tarde.

And the third. Drive home from the sea. Easy parking on 6th. Walk to Spring and see them, wild and laughing. Fangs and teeth with gray in their scruff. What it is to have brothers/ how easy they are to embrace/ to sink into. Drink and walk the summer winding down only now, your bare legs feeling the city's chill. But coyotes, the hillside gasps. But your familiar. A lit hearth, the howling outside. Take attendance: every beating heart accounted for, even those in absence. Even the dreams that come across the sea and after weeks: in the dark/ what is known/ how we know/ how we reach in half-sleep and remember the lights left on, the leaves swaying with hello. How the wilderness welcomes home the animals that roost. And what relief, to stand and not sit, to breath the hillside's breath and not exhaust, to reach for soft clothes and all my animals.

Fridays are the longest. Up in a lavender dark, too stiff and cold, the hot water and lemon, the whining calico. and going west, to the sea. Past the train tracks where Chiwan goes to his mother's and where once you watched a hawk land on a pigeon. You stared as the pigeon flailed but turned away before the first terrible bite.

What it is to feel ill in a crowd. To sit in an empty room waiting for it to pass. You are nauseous till it passes. You are sleepy till it passes. You are cold. The cold does not pass.

Go to a place with a tree growing indoors. But there is no cat. Or at least not one that you can see. A dream is remembered and recounted. A coven, a pack, is present. And after, the glitter sidewalks and squeezing into a diner booth like when you were young.

Eldest was born. Bad of eyes tall in the skin. What it was to have bad eyes back then.

[Nov 16]

Fell asleep. Sister woke me up to say goodbye. She left and I was too sleepy to check the doors. The rats or whatever, upstairs.

Left the lights on. At 6:30 the sun was out – the slight chill, my pajamas too thin to keep my knees warm.

The calico looking for the lynx.

La muerte de Ernestina (remember to ask your mom).

9:55 on a platform no trains no (illegible).

The machine that screeched along the rails cleaning sounded exactly like a kitchen dragging a village behind it.

All of the yucatecos. Dtla. Train. Walk to library, then to bar.

Drunk on the train platform you make acquaintance w Flora. Flora trying to get to Lancaster, her brother died, she says. Her red flower. White people are so mean she says.

Lovers on the train not so young smile and try not to stare but really I stare.

[Nov 22] walk out w calico/the morning still damp.

Rachel/the birds
Them/the hurricane
The mistake of the motorcycle
Feel the feel
The difference between and being
Language performance
mother, country
mother/country
We call the hour bird o clock.

And then the awful day of thanks, attendance taken by your mother. You are here my eldest. Attend.

A Friday you go again to the west, but this time to bring home the stray fox. How happy you are to hold her and listen to her adventures.

Around town the firs are showing up, the fibrous boughs and garlands. You watch neighbors leave pine needles on the street. You wear thin cotton and no shoes and you hold a steaming cup on your porch.

The last day of the month meet Rachel and name names.

Cempazúchitl 1

Oh net of rhizomes oh labyrinth oh open door oh eternity /
velvet corolla sepal a gold a path
what is there to go back for in a place eaten by wind/
everything is sand.
campo santo:
wrought iron painted pink and poured concrete.
Junkies or someone break the glass
and steal the rosary, the virgin, the cherub.
Somewhere a pawn shop, a patrol car,
a sad mother is a place for those things,
some dashboard, some niche, some mouth waits
for communion.

Cempazúchitl 2

Astacae (mature flower)
Petal: corolla/
a lantern in the cold bitter
here, pollinator, your fur and scruff,
your hum and pinch.
The last throes, a heat.
Bare legs walk toward heat
and then run toward fangs/
the hour of the predator/ the familiar.
(they call it incentive)
Function and the purpose of the petal
an operation/ a reason (to be seen)
landed on, velvet scallops/ how the gentle tug
releases the corn silk tails.

altars everywhere

(this is not a poem about pan dulce or tamales or abuela or Guadalupe or/or/or)
how to build a place to land on/ pollinator come/
the wasp or/or/or:
The sting of theft
a twinge while sleep comes/*comes for who*/
the thin veil: *neblina*/
as beaded curtains, as cave of lanterns (little soul, little light).
Stubborn girl: you never come when called
you never come.

Tunnel

And then December comes
as dead bay leaves/
a tunnel to the main line,
The early days before a pilgrimage of red brocade,
Mother offering you to the fanged serpent you call MOTHER.
In the north, the winter is dry and hot;
Oranges fall, untouched.
A dead mouse and two dead trees later
comes the sea, the wall of salt water
and then the soothing/ the small hand/ warm breath.
Where is the compass the way home—
the banks of bruised citrus turning over my cells
nowhere, pilgrim:
a valley of a kind,
An idyll. Wild.
That place was never there.

[1 December] Hawks again today, one redtail pink gliding up the current stirring that air mass in and over the Hahamongna. Air mass that comes down the mountain from the San Gabriels and down the hill by JPL. And one, flying into the high end of La Tuna Canyon, not a redtail I don't think. A cooper's, maybe, wanting to be high like that; a sharp-shinned wouldn't want to be so far out of the canopy. There *is* canopy there, pooling in the steep tiny canyon washes all up and down the larger La Tuna Canyon topography. Also pigeons in a flutter of light white and light gray, east of Lincoln. Southbound on the 267 I see them spin tail feathers up.

[2] the fuck am I thinking, these days, redacted; it's good to see them last night but fuck me I could not get still. For the life of me, vibrating out of my skins. The birds were on their way to bed... The forecast for the foothill high plain said, wind. And wind it was. Windy the *alta dena*. A high hummingbird in the tree that loses leaves and gets the red clusters that look like blossoms but might be *which lover are you jack of diamonds* might be a different cluster of leaves. No hawks in sight, in my sight anyway, and gusting pushes of wind, slow and strong and again hasty and blowing so soft. Monice's book on my *mind!* A crow stroking quick wing; wind; a set of parrots, wind; a passle—a line-up—of pigeons on the *Sunday morning at the diner Hollywood trembles on the verge of tears* on the lip of the parking deck overlooking the park. Scared still, the money, the nightmare.

December spreads out like Scout on the wooden floor: pancake batter. I finish edits for Monice's book and think about the letter I'll write her. Rocío reads at Poetic Research Bureau and I see how she stands and speaks; did it take me a long time to hear the inflections when she reads aloud? How differently I know her body and voice now. What kind of mammal witch am I writing with, to and fro. Early in 2010 I read excerpts of her poetry; redacted; her voice on the phone for two hours, pacing in the grocery store; meeting in person; redacted; driving down the 110 and across the 105 to teach; hearing her read her work; redacted. Attendance has been a seven year jubilee, maybe.

[5] a picture of the new puppy at Hannah's job

[6] Sarah sends me a foto of their cat Percy come in from the rain, wrapped entirely up in a pink towel

[7] Glowing sky on the way home, warm on the near empty bus, cool on the roof with the bamboo starlings, first quarter moon. Me and Rocío.

[8] a picture of a Hannah with a different dog at her job

[9] a foto of Ruth's bunny rabbit. Later I will learn what is a prey animal, what it means to pick up a rabbit from above or pull it out from under a hiding place. Prey animals are wired differently, I learn

the OWL *before* twilight powerful flies from over the arroyo near the rose bowl, towards the dam and the watershed. Lands *you you needed me* lands at the top of a long-needled pine, giant.

[10] a party, I go at all because I said I'd meet Nicole and Nona. I talk all night to G. (Later I forget we went home together.) I think about touch, and how people keep dogs, and how Zoë writes

[11] Sarah sends a picture of their black cat Oskar perched on the trash can, trying to get in on the action in the kitchen. And one of Oskar playing in the washer and dryer. I accept these now

[12] Sarah sends an image of a piece of paper with "Time of death 8:05" written on it, right when she goes on shift in the MICU. Another picture of a bunny hiding on a bookshelf. Julia lives there now so I resign myself

[14] A picture of Percy sprawled on Sarah and Peter's couch. Another picture of the new puppy at Hannah's job. There are like six dogs at her office now, even with the fotos it's hard to be exact

[16] Alice's. We go through pictures of her as a little girl creature. She's waiting for her little creature to come—one more month.

[17] Sarah is a bridesmaid for Kaitlyn's winter wedding. She send a LOT of fotos of Kaitlin's white Westie dog. "Guys. All my dreams have come true. I'm in a hotel with Wendell."

[18] My mom is going through some of Sarah's random stuff stored in the H's garage basement. Julia is making her. She sends fotos of fotos: a drawing of a cat that little kid Sarah made, I think from an art class when we still lived in Black Mountain. I think I understand people and their animals but I probably don't. It's been more than 15 years since Katie died. Is that real? The pictures sent of Sarah and Maryahm playing dress up don't make me cry but how is it possible that I have to do the math to remember it would have been the year before her mom was murdered

—

Ravens, pigeons, hawks. (Parrots.) Small human creature bodies at school. So many 5150s. I know the brain is like a jellyfish, I know it, I can feel it and each nerve is a tendril of the organism being, and there is grey matter in our fingertips. (What other animals does this apply to?) In scar tissue, trauma tissue, how traumatized brains light up in scans; how do our brain tendrils look, trauma all lit up? (Fingers slammed in the car door.)

We plan on fire for solstice.

Attending is bleeding out of me. This is the year to notice how strangely I attend—hyperfocused or not at all. It's not the environmental scanning I used to do, sitting with my eyes on the exits, back to the wall. Setting up my tarp with a specific relationship to the feeling of a campsite's topography and to sightlines towards each of my students. Not only that. It's a soupy drift. My friends *please just look me in my face* notice. Even in public space, times of un-focus while I walk in the world with my body, though our posture habits are still a clear fuckoff. (And it is privilege to slacken, even slightly, the constant assessment of threat and vulnerability.) The sharp incursions of men startle me but there's a new anger that shimmers first and burns later.

In therapy we talk about money.

Rocío and I have wandered out into the world and a shared interiority. We begin to walk back into the rooms of flora and fauna, we begin to shift our connectedness.

The sound of the raven's wings, their pinions moving across one another, that is the year. With Zoë a year ago in the desert I heard *the raven the raven the noise of its wings in flight* and during the year the sound became audible through the city air too. (On Epiphany, again, together with Rocío, again, together.)

a year like this passes so strangely somewhere between sorrow and bliss

—

[18] Bird o'clock, alone, not.

[19] More fotos from storage: A nativity drawn "12/17/97 by Julia + Sarah." The sheep are talking to each other and one of them yells at the other to be quiet. It's a direct quote from our dad, if you substitute "trying to get some peace and quiet" for "trying to listen to the angels"

[20] Solstice attendance, just about right-right. The cats. Our humans come. Jen brings Zizi and gives him her skin. Afterwards me and Rocío clean up and sit with Ana around the fire I spread to coal bed so it starts to cool down. *and you swimming up tide or just tuning in radio stations* For some reason I think about Theandrew's birthday, ten days away. No I know the reason, it's the fire, so many nights at FP with his face, playing music off his phone by the fire *I left my love in a field*

[23] "Poor Oskar has conjunctivitis" foto. If I tallied every cat picture this year, between Sarah and Rocío... how do I attend to that? I never feel like I give the desired response. Pets are weird because they die differently than people. Maybe

[24] In transit, a picture of Sarah and Percy getting ready for bed; a picture of Oskar sniffing a trapped roach

—

There are many hibernations in December and I'm not sure they count as hummingbird torpor. There is not very much writing in the moment and there are not very many bird o'clocks. I'm in avoiding. *you're given me a million reasons, about a million reasons, giving me a million reasons I bow down and pray I try to make the worst feel better lord show me the way to cut through all this worn out leather* I see Rogue One with my dad.

I wonder why it's only now I'm writing in my family and our attendance.

—

[25] Walk by the French Broad River, sun gone down, brown and grey rivaling a desert palette subtlety. With Julia and Laura. Mom comes home and puts on the Staples Sisters. Dances.

[26] the Feast of St. Stephen: Walk down along by Hominy Creek, bigger than I remember, off of Sulphur Springs Road. With Julia and Mom.

[28] Walk down by the river again, this time with Mom. The sun hasn't quite gone behind the ridge when we get there but it's biting cold. The animals are hidden out of my sensing range, except a thrush bird.

[28] Amber shows me the cartoon portrait Sadie drew of Lola, the cat who left her last year. Animals go off to die, that's what we learned growing up

[29] More cat pictures. I have the car and take it up to the Tennessee line. There's a raven and it flies off. I spend time looking at the paper wasp nest in the redbud tree. From up there you can see how the Black Mountain range falls from northwest to east. Hannah plays and sings for me

[30] Julia gets a flat tire on the way to Chattanooga. She sends fotos of articles in the Clay County newspaper about the "famously bizarre Possum Drop" for New Years Eve in Brasstown. There's another article about an elderly woman over in Cherokee, something about how the county didn't realize she had died; it's titled, "Check the Obits." Check the obits—my grandmother's form of attending these days.

—

I go down by the river and watch the train. I take my mom when she has to work and listen to the 5:00 a.m. bluegrass show on the way back to sleep on Pacific Standard Time. I am from here more than anywhere else I am. I just turn into time space goop and I don't know how to feel like a person when we're all this close together. I don't write and barely read.

Later Zoë's writing affect feels around my writing again. It's so cold in my mom's studio and I take to sleeping under my mom's fur coat, this giant fur from my grandmother Sheehan, who knows what decade. Fur is like, magic. I didn't know.

you you needed me Breakfast all four of us sisters, how we are.

—

[1 January] Hannah and I finish rehearsing

[2] right at dark, the train down by the river. We've rehearsed our show and now Hannah plays and sings, I read, we talk. *Listening Downstream*, we call it

[3] Our walk up the Blue Ridge Parkway takes us by Rattlesnake Lodge ("remember that summer we hiked there and there was that baby rattler on the trail, and Janet would not leave that spot, she was determined to guard us all") and two of the tunnels built by the Civilian Conservation Corps, and the view over Bull Creek Valley where a white settler named Joseph Rice killed "the last buffalo seen in this locality" in 1799. *do you remember I feel that you remember you choose not to remember I think it is the know it is the bad bad blood* Later I think of friends growing up out on Riceville Road and wonder at how the bloodletters divided up the lands and named them. Mom and I only startle once, a big noise in the brush down the north slope below us. We halt. We wait... Another sound doesn't come.

[4] Tea with Rachel and hello to her good dog, her lovely good black dog. Rachel, I don't know how to talk about. It's beautiful out. Tea with Amber; the familiar and chaos spirit.

[5] Landing in Los Ángeles there is the wondrous cloud sky sundown

Feast of Epiphany

Hiking La Tuna Canyon with Rocío. I love that we keep our quiet together. The three ravens playing the air at the ridge right above us. Us, stopped at a switchback turn exposed to the sun, looking out towards the San Fernando Valley and, to our north, the mountains. The last raven and its feathers, for that moment the only sound, the only movement. The dry-oiled black pinion feathers sealed against fraying, scraping lightly across one another, flexing over a pulsing of muscle and ligature and blooded-ness. On the way down, the splayed white-bone sycamore.

The datura drowned in the green *breaking into unbelievable breath.*

And always finally pigeons, who mean when they appear: That when humans nurture and then cast out, there is a trace. Pigeon palomas, doves, spirits, dirty with grit. Still here, how long, maybe as long as we are here.

December

Here it comes. The kitchen/the village.

The first day on a Thursday. Dark so early/lose count of lights.

Mountains/Pasadena/ocean/hillside. This wilderness, I tell you (tell who?).

A long sit, the long fade. Make me lavender, you said to her. Make me the color of the wilderness, of the cold dark.

The garden of red light, the cold and polar bear shirt. You named the names and people politely heard you do it. And after? No one remembers but there are pictures to prove it.

On the porch, the chill in your knees. Your ankle. A hawk so early, in place of your crows.

oh ankle, oh scar, oh birthmark.

(early leaves were quick to fall *but last leaves hang on*)

A morning: the line of a back/ the breathing. A valley of enemies.

the dig and drag. a clay soil choking the bay laurels/the bay laurel roots choking the hundred-year-old clay pipes. a hollow in the jungle, like a sink hole. like the earth just swallowed somebody. maybe a bratty kid. the workers make a great noise for many hours. finches watch from dead branches.

Office hours- a meta attendance? got to dt, stop for tacos. sit at Tony P's. Ask for the elder (she is on vacation). Eat so much. forget why thursday you don't go outside at all.

Friday: the dark in the morning/ slow to leave.

anticipate the long day sea side but not by the sea. outside the wind whips at the path.

Saturday we clambered up the narrow staircase with glasses of champagne or prosecco or whatever and waffles. We reclined in chairs and the sun made us laugh. We walked the corgi and the eye wandered to plants easy for stealing. you are always just stealing.

And after- to pourhaus. Our awful conversations, the flight of wines. *flight.* as if we could escape. the scowl of you wants to punish, but you have no punishment to give.

The north pole is so far away, but ruben and alex live nearby. A sad sister (this is not my life/it's just a fond farewell to a friend.

The quiet city, you drive past even pilgrims. Even pilgrims and their brass bands, their children in linens and braids, they don't make a sound. Was it Hill or Alameda; did you turn your face left or right to catch her song, to say her name in the tongue your mother kept hidden in plain sight. Here are five questions, on a slip of paper in your hand: Am I not here who am your Mother? Are you not under my shadow and protection? Am I not your fountain of life? Are you not in the folds of my mantle? In the crossing of my arms? Is there anything else you need?

mother my muse/imagine her turning to you and saying she has decided something. how firm her small fists. on the twelfth day (your mother gives to you).
when traci asks about november, you remember.

Whittier: transport large sacks of succulents. work the damp soil. how nicely they take. how quickly you work. how good the soil. dark, good soil. the lynx so happy he races around.

late to mother's feet. ya llegué madre. tarde, pero ya vine. little banners wave, make shadows on her face. instrucciones: go to the third stall on the left. pass under the petticoats of communion gowns. The lace catches strands of your hair. Reach for torso over the glass case of precious wares, the life-size christ child with synthetic eyelashes. his plump hands and fluted fingers. Weeks later, standing at the barre with your arm overhead, you will make your hands this way. This is the kind of deliverance you seek.

You come home with a new clay somerio and copal beads, a new rebozo. You cover and uncover yourself in the mirror, looking for traces of your women-folk. here, her eyes. here, her nose. How they scurried home under black thundering clouds as the fat drops of water fell. how they ran at first light to a sweetheart, to a road, to a compass pointing north.

and solstice. and fire. men's voice (our brothers, at the mouth of a wilderness. and then a lit hearth and a full home. this is correct. mother bathes her family in smoke. mother leads the family through the paths in the dark, crushing the citrus leaf, the lavender flower.

and the hangover the next day. it has not stopped raining since. You are summoned to Tony's on seventh. you do math in glasses of whiskey, you dance and sing and play with the beads around your neck. black and blue pictures tell you how it went. black and white pictured show you yourselves.

in the wet night only small lights register. when you were small, you didn't know you couldn't see. you liked the hazy cluster of colored pearls you saw out of the car window. it was beautiful. an eve: in the morning, loading up the car to head for the border, your father looks at you and says "don't drink so much".

instrucciones: drive east. snow so close. sleep so much. and then cross into baja california. you cross that river, the egrets stalking/ their fancy walk.

the roads are all mud, deep wells where others crossed before you. you sink up to your ankles. the ground is kissing you as you walk, is making kissing sounds. the rooms you stay in are cold, but at least no spiders this time.

botas de siete leguas. all those years ago, the old dragon would laugh at your scuffed boots. and he laughed with you too. you were clever and valuable. he rolled up his pant leg to show you his twin birthmark. only we two, little dragon. you were proud of your mean look, the scowl line that divided your forehead since you looked in a mirror.

(remember on the drive, there was a tree, in Indio- the curious bird in the curious tree?)

an aunt, a spotted dog. the last of Maura's bougainvillea. eldest and youngest in the crumbling home of my dead grandmother. your mother is everything to them now. they speak gently to her. the touch her hands. the haruspex/augur in her bed, small as a lily. her birds set free, given away or eaten. "Rocío siempre tan discreta" she says to your sister. she asks after her familiar and you fetch him my looking out the window. "*tonchi, men, men*," you coax, in a language no one knows. he hears her voice in your voice; this is comforting. She handed you the knife once. she turned hens inside out to show you the spring's approach once. once, the one you call alpha in this house bid you help bathe the haruspex/augur. care for the temple, priestess. be in service of creation, priestess. be the handmaiden of this place, of this living light.

you were silent in the bath, lifting her hair and pouring warm water. you let alpha cluck and chatter to her. alpha said to you: how many times did she heal our bodies. how many times did she comfort our sorrows.

somewhere, the children shriek in delight of candy, and fire. remember those glorious nights of making fires unsupervised. (it was only a movie/ I was so young then).

your breath hangs in front of you as tea leaves. never minimize the luxury of a hot shower.

how dark the desert.

and the lights in the west. you take off your glasses to see what you saw, to remember yourself.

the gaping hole in the coffee table in the middle of the living room in the middle of the house in the middle of 60th street in the middle of a map that no one ever drew.

Except, your body is a map. the gaping hole is in your belly. the absence. that vacancy. your mother's nativity scene without the infant because she doesn't remember where she put it. perhaps you have just misplaced your children.

it's fine. it's fine. she is happy. not just okay, but happy. everything is wonderful.

there is a party. A baby is held. poinsettias in decorative mylar bright as the red light. in the rain you watched a tribe assemble. you miss them, the absent. you take attendance of your beloved. when the rain clears, everyone will be present.

indoor plants die in over-watered pots, but there is so much to drink. a clock ticks, the hour strikes. mouth reach, mouth open. the first word of the year is silent, is made.

A pearl, a harbor.

Once, *shown the pomegranate/the chambers,*
The haruspex proclaims (almost a mother).
To who was she speaking?
Broken-hearted (as pomegranates or
blackberries or split birds) at her responsibility
she separates fascia from muscle and gristle.
Little priestess/ take this knife. In this house
you have never been eldest. But here comes death,
priestess (tuck us in your cheek for later priestess).
how pomegranates smash at thresholds/
how wet you get at the idea.

Nochebuena

Little daughter (of)
envoys in ships in sashes
what the word
indigenous is (we didn't have
that word we didn't need it)
false flower in that petals
are leaves in other colors
that kind of red/ for lovers
for passions come too soon
(happy birthday; here comes resurrection)
In twelve hours (how dark, the desert,
the night you scurried north).

Pilgrim, again

We just missed each other
Late late or was it early early.
What colors are in words like
Amanecer, madrugada, the insides of shells
of your young thighs.
Young skywalker, I am not as young as your others
But find this temple and wash your weary mind here
(small blooms, crushed the long night of fire, flare)
In the canopies of old magnolias, doves feign sleep.
You, you come for the fire-making. You stay for the wilderness.

an after attendance

future somatics to do list
[*a love letter to attendance: to rachel and rocío*]

is negative space the only kind of space?

what is the name for air that does not shimmer?

which gaps can be tasted?

who are we to say?

(jp said *we is not nosotrxs.*)

(no one will be the teacher or everyone will be the teacher or there is nothing to teach and everything to learn.)

who are we not to say?

what can we actually unlearn?

what color is the time it takes to prepare for the time to disappear or flare in a blaze of undone momentum?

capitalism is cellular where birdsound is molecular?

moving into and out of stasis or just being in a state?

our context is torrent? our teacher is to welcome?

birdsong is molecular where pores concentrically expand?

into and out of heresy?

(no, hearsay: what we said after we heard what was available when we listened. capacious. conscientious. license.)

the porous and filled space between persons is atomic?

(exactitude is not a virtue. nor is virtue.)

how to live inside an attendant we without knowing too much?

(z calls palomas "pamolas" and the autobús "aubotús.")

emptiness fills? frills, cilia, or what happens to the undigestible?

attending translates witness to wonder? and minute specific
exacting declaration inexactly? but more gentle, without
whisper? not without wish?

shall we abandon the impulse to overtake? shall we slough off
layers of administration to expose the medular hollow?

(the city sags under the heft of the revitalization of its already
vital neighborhoods.)

where might we rest our heads?

- jen hofer, 2018

acknowledgements

We would like to acknowledge Chiwan Choi and Cultural Weekly for publishing excerpts of *Attendance* throughout 2016. We didn't know it at the time, but having the work appear in the world as it appeared in the world became an attendance all its own. Thank you, Chiwan.

We thank our families. We thank Traci Kato-Kiriyama and the Tuesday Night Cafe family; Say Her Name / A Requiem for Sandra Bland series family; Jessica Ceballos y Campbell, Peter Woods, Avenue 50, Las Lunas Locas, Karineh Mahdessian, Bridgette Bianca, Janice Lee, Melora Walters, Louise Mathias, F. Douglas Brown, Rihanna; Jen Hofer and Antena; Skira Martinez, Paul Vangelisti, Amy Orazio and family, Dennis Phillips, Nicole Fiore, Judeth Oden Choi, Ana Chaidez, 90x90 and Writ Large Press; St. James in the City and Martha Ronk for music; Starlings, Tullamore Dew; Elæ [Lynne DeSilva-Johnson] and The Operating System; Los Ángeles, the River, the Appalachian Mountains, Sonny's, the cats, Alice Astourian, Zoë Ruiz, Amber Church, Eva Chavez, C.D. Wright, P-22, Monice Mitchell Simms, Brande Jackson, Rebecca Lee; Theandrew's community; Teka Lark Lo, Winona Leon, Moa Junström, tk lê, Kirsten Giles, the Sheridan family, Angelina Favre; WilSkills and Pisgah National forest wilderness instructors; Lynn Wadsworth, Sierra Nicole Qualles, Emily Heath Connor; Ashaki Jackson and Surveillance; Jane Anderson, India Radfar, librecht baker, Amelia Greenhall, Katie Wagman, Sarah Stephens, Sarah Brooks, Claire Brown, Natashia Deón, Jaquita Ta'le, Dae Jung, Kate Maruyama, Never Angeline Nørth and Meteor (may she lay us waste).

poetics and process:
elæ (lynne desilva-johnson) with
rocío carlos and rachel mcleod kaminer

Welcome! Thank you so much for taking the time to talk with us today.
Can you each introduce yourself in the way that you would choose?

RMK: Hi, I'm Rachel! She/her. Nice to see you! Idk what else to say jaja. I'm a person? It's an honour? Srsly though. Thank you, Elæ.

RC: I'm Rocío. She/her/them/they. Thanks for having us!

When did you decide you were a poet (and/or: do you feel comfortable calling yourself a poet, what other titles or affiliations do you prefer/feel are more accurate)?

RC: Poet is a good word for what I do, personally. I'd say I was about fourteen when I realized I made poems. I was like oh shit, this can't be good.

RMK: I think "poet" is the weirdest word ever and I always kind of get this wiggle-flinch feeling about it. But in a good way. Like a cool reminder that the reason I don't feel totally comfortable is that there's something ancient and primal going on with poetry. Don't play with fire unless you're willing to play with fire I guess?
I'm a "reader," I think.

In what ways, forms, and materials does your creative process manifest itself?

RC: Writing is like my metabolism. I can't go too long without thinking about it or making some of it or I will become irritable and frustrated. And yet I sometimes go for long periods of time without doing it. Sometimes I have had to join up with friends and carve out group time for prompts. Once, I resorted to taking on crazy student debt just to be in graduate school and have a deadline. This is an oversimplification but you get the idea. I will sometimes write notes and ideas by hand and then transcribe them into word processing documents. Lately I ramble into my notes app to tease out later. As far as form, my particular conventions are pretty normalized at this point, in terms of the use of space, line breaks and punctuation. But I often think of threads of voices floating over each other. This, in my upcoming book (*the other house*) is as close to form as I've ever gotten.

Attendance came from a specific prompt we gave ourselves, but that prompt (to notice, note and annotate) is just an extension of our personal tendencies to "attend."

RMK: Honestly, idk how to answer this these days. There is a lot of hibernation involved. The physical act of writing has always been really important, whether it turns into a written "piece" or not. Sometimes writing is a way to hold space with myself. Looking back to the years building up to my first book I can see sparks that come from (or are sustained by) structure and problem-solving, etymology, idioms and proverbs, holy books, nature and natural history–the story we are telling ourselves about the world. Um, love? And heartbreak of all kinds. And of course, notation.

A lot of *Attendance* was taking my well-worn practices and knowing they needed to eat themselves up. Idk what's left or what's next, but I know I've changed.

I like the word "experiment."

What's a "poet", anyway?

RC: Well since Poet is a weird word in that it conjures a specific kind of person having permission to speak, in a specific way, it's hard to be the person who "gate-keeps" what a poet can be. A poet is whomever decides she is a poet.

RMK: A poet is a self-identified poet.

What is the role of the poet today / what do you see as your cultural and social role (in the poetry community and beyond)? What other work are you doing in the world and how does it interface with your creative practice at this time?

RC: Again, to prescribe a thing or role for the poet in the position of gate-keeping feels weird… In the world I teach for a living. At the schools where I work I challenge the paradigms of western-ness or white-settler culture "first-ness" or "most-ness" if that makes sense. In my neighborhood I pay attention to plants and animals (I belong to my cats and my backyard, to the street and the hillside and chaparral and the sierra).This contemplative/devotional part of my day is instrumental to my practice. Annually, I volunteer as a "camp counselor" at a girls' rock camp. Rachel and I also publish a yearly chapbook under the name 'wirecutter collective.' These two things fulfill the "community" or "good works" part of being a poet as I live it. My idea of being a poet is of being as of/in the world as much as it is being in solitude. My poetics cannot be separate from my desperation to survive. Also, in my world, to be a poet is to take up space and make room to pull others through.

It's so strange—I read that [interface with your work] as "INTERFERE," so I say the following: The "teacher" part of my life can at times take up my resources: time, drive, energy. In that role, I hope to create opportunities for students to wonder and build and revise and tear down. But make no mistake, it is exhausting. For now I can say that in the classroom workshop setting, each time I myself wonder, alongside my students, about poetry, I clarify and illuminate something.

RMK: Lol I am at a serious crossroads with this. I recently exited the non-profit industrial complex (again) and entered the for-profit industrial complex (again) (as if they are separate) so that's a whole thing (again).

This poet's life is in the world. Chosen family – and I thank my fucking stars that I got to choose some of my family of origin for that – and community, neighborhood, city, world. There is a jump there that skips US states and the US nation-state, not in a holier-than-thou way; I just really don't think that is an orientation I personally can sustain. Which is funny because a couple of my sisters are strongly committed to un-fucking our home state (North Carolina) and I'm so grateful. Also I think being in the world includes the internet and also being alone. Um where was this going?? Oh:

A poet is to be a person and a neighbor. So like I don't think art-making and writing and self-expression and publication are in and of themselves are good. At the moment. I do believe they are powerful, always: the blade always has two edges, the curse carries its own blessing, the superpower exacts a price on the world around. Amoral and feral and caring and real.

So the role of a poet is to write and be a person diving deep into the work-that-is-real and then sometimes judiciously making your writing public? Idk. There's also being a fuck yeah! person for every writer you meet who isn't comfortable fully claiming it. I think the role of a poet is to be like Yes! You are a writer! That is what this is! Um it might not be "good" but keep writing and reading and listening and doing the thing!

How did you meet and become collaborators? What made you want to work together?

RC: I met Rachel over the phone. I was on my way out of a grad program and she was considering her options. Next thing you know we got to know each other as carpool buddies, and after the program got together with other graduates to keep writing. Eventually people left town or drifted from the group and only she and I were left. I don't know how we decided to do this exactly. Or how we ended up at that bar on that night and wrote a plan on a napkin.

RMK: Paul Vangelisti called me and offered me a place at Otis. He knew I should talk to Rocío. I called her (omg what a versatile little millenial I am!) and we spoke for like two hours. You know that thing where you are at the grocery store and get on the phone and can't pay attention, so you just walk the aisles til the call is over? Yeah.

The thing about the grad school we went to is that it wasn't a complete experience—by design. I didn't want another residential undergrad experience where the bubble pops and suddenly you and all your partners-in-crime are on four continents. (And Rocío told me, yes, people work and go to school at the same time here.) I wanted to find out if I could live in a place. (Los Ángeles is not exactly a place, but ok.) And I knew, always, that it was a rare and special invitation that Rocío extended to me. That this place was in so many ways *hers* and I was entering a space she made for me in her life.

Um that is a lot of our first instant together. Suffice it to say our relationship grew fast and grew slow—and we separately and together nurtured community—and a few years later there we were. One thing connecting us has always been the natural world, including the city world.

Talk about the process of making this work, both independently and together. Did you have this intention or develop the idea for a while? What en- couraged and/or confounded this (or a book, in general) coming together? What was unexpected or surprising, if anything, about the process? How did it change or evolve?

RC: This answer begins where the last question left off. We were in a bar, conspiring to make something and choosing our constraint. We had arrived at this after being out of school and Rachel had finished *As in the dark, descend*, and I suppose the boring human part of this is that we were like "now what?" But also, we were just talking, just trying to be humans "person-ing" in the world. Which is to say "poet." And to attend had been such a natural action for each of us, in our own way.

So then there was this napkin…
We drew up deadlines and lanes (mine was flora, Rachel's was fauna) and then proceeded to ignore them. Well not right away, and not entirely. The idea was to take notes and then make poems. But then we were like woah woah woah when do the notes end and the work begin. And also the world crept in. Rachel's observance of the birds in the thicket could not ignore the bamboo thicket where they nested. My observance of the springtime flowering could not be without desire and bodies. And neither of us could ignore The Drought.

RMK: What she said! No but really. We totally knew we wouldn't stay in our lanes. My question from the outset was "when do the notes for the work become the work." And later, "well what did we think was going to happen." Is that true Rocío?

RC: Did we know? I feel like I was tired in December 2015, when we conceived it. I mean. IDK. Probably? I mean it makes sense. How could I not write about Scout? That seems crazy.

RMK: Okay so the process: It was surprising but—I feel naked about this in the book—I wanted to be writing on purpose. That sounds weird but like. I want to start from a point of overt knowing and travel from there. *As in the dark, descend* started from a place of not-knowing and (with a LOT of time) moved to a place of un-knowing. I also was at this point of knowing how to write a "rachel" poem, and I needed to stop knowing how. The amount of time writing and revising was the "pressure" that transformed it into a book. Ugh this sounds sooooo fancy but truly truly I mean this in the least meta/process-y way possible. It's just what was true for me in 2016. Instead of time + revision as the transforming pressure, it was deadlines + letting go of revision.

Now I've/we've come back to the place of putting a book into the world, and I'm fucking lost in space again. Not in a deep interesting way, jaja, just in a normal well-shit kind of way.

Writing with a companion was transformative for me as a reader and a "poet-colleague" (to borrow the word of poet Amy Orazio). To be honest I have no fucking clue how to "explain" some of Rocío's work in this book. I couldn't say for sure what she's talking about, and that is LIBERATING. There are feelings, and then there is my personal experience of the music of the language, and then there is the magic of re-reading and re-listening.

RC: Well, ditto.

This work was produced around a formal concept or guiding experimental principle. Was that a new way of working for each of you, or is this indicative of your practice in other ways?

RMK: I am super super into constraint. Jaja ask Rocío about our conversations re: ballet. At the same time… I said earlier that I knew my "well-worn practices needed to eat themselves up." So wherever you go, there you are—never not constraint—but by the second half of Attendance I thought I might be moving away from it. And yeah no, now I have no idea, but at least Attendance made this an open question again.

RC: I also love a constraint, but only when they feel right. And they can feel right even if they're painful. But I had only done it alone before. It was new to write with/for someone. I have to say

I'm hooked. I want to do it all the time now. Even an ekphrastic poem is a poem with and for someone else.

RMK: Oh ya. Definitely have no idea how to write alone. (Scared about that.) But also extremely sure that writing alone isn't really a thing.

RC: Agreed.

As we get deeper into Attendance, *your voices become interchangeable, so that the audience isn't necessarily aware after a certain juncture which of you has written / is speaking the words they receive. Can you talk about the decision to and practice of integrating each of your independent processes into a manuscript that felt "finished"?*

How did you go about the editorial process in this case? Do the poems represent words that were part of the original act of attending or were they developed collaboratively from documentary text that started in a different form? Would it be possible to see the process through incremental edits in any way? It could be interesting for the audience to see how a page or pages evolved, how your voices combined, were parsed and edited to become what we see now.

RMK: You know, there were moments where we were inexplicably writing about the same things. On accident, so to speak. And it would be so cool! Like omg I can't believe we both used the same words this month! But *Attendance* is also a reminder about magical thinking—that clichè that the reason you and your friend call each other at the same instant is that you are listening to the same radio station and "your song" comes on and you both hear it. Connection is mysterious and magical but also *it's not that deep*. And that is so cool!!! That you can lean into magical thinking while being in a very ambiguous relationship with Meaning and The Universe and Spirit.

As far as the voice-blending and the revision—there was so much trust involved. Again, not in a deep way. A very matter of fact trust, like "yup, cool, here we go." Interpersonally it was a deep year, but the writing/reading was the space where we connected no matter what. I think—Rocío what is your feel?

RC: Poetry can be close quarters and I suppose we adopted each other's lexicons and our friend-vernacular crept in. And every month we read each other's notes and so some of that literally made it into each other's months, the way you tell someone about a line you read or a scene you watched. My drafts of the entire year are printed, highlighted and marked up with Rachel's brilliant feedback. Also she has such lovely hand-writing.

RMK: Okay but very literally: We shared each month's "notes" as we each embarked on writing that month's "poems." Then we shared the next month's "poems" as we each wrote the next month's "notes." So in that sense it was a very obvious way of influencing one another's content and voice and style and subject and whatever else. To be honest I think the voices can be quite estranged at times—in my mind there's an imaginary re-reader who spends lots and lots of time with the book and in the end, this imaginary re-reader has a definitive idea of who wrote what and is extremely incorrect but also correct.

Jaja I like the word "embarked" because early on we talked a lot about the notes as the "captain's log." Also lol @ you using the word feedback, I feel like the appropriate F words here are "feeling" and "fangirling."

What formal structures or other constrictive practices (if any) do you use in the creation of your work? Have certain teachers or instructive environments, or readings/writings of other creative people (poets or others) informed the way you work/write? Whose work or presence in the world is really influencing you or your work right now? Can you talk a little bit about why?

RC; Well first and foremost was the way my parents spoke at home and reported on their day and asked about mine and my sister's. Then there was the actual going outside. Someone would say "let's go outside!" and the four of us would stand in our little yard in South East L.A. and talk about the plants. My parents grew up pretty rural and called every plant by name. It was so specific, perfect for a poet. They were never like, "go sit under that tree," but always "sit under the mesquite." Since there really isn't that kind of education for a person available here in the states (you have to be a nerd to know all the names of all the trees growing on your street), I still mostly know only the Spanish or even indigenous (nahuatl) names for some plants. Like I had to look up huamúchil, which is from the nahuatl cuahmotchitl to find out it's a Madras Thorn in English. Shrug emoji?

It's strange to know the names of things but have them mean something totally different in English, and here in the North. For example the flower Alcatráz is a Calla Lily (the name is Spanish Arabic) but here it is always a famous prison. An Alamo is a Poplar tree, but here it only means that fort where my parents' country was at war with this country.

As far as reading: the daybooks of Robert Crosson contained all the minutiae of a day: the people who came and went, who called on the telephone, the body and the memory of desire, tangents about culture. That's one. Claudia Rankine's Citizen and its collection of small daily agressions and survivals. Bhanu Kapil's *Humanimal's* written wonder and the body and the forest.

And now, lately, I'm noticing a lot of writings that explore otherness through the device of artificial intelligence or machinery, like Margaret Rhee's *Love, Robot*, Franny Choi's *Death by Sex Machine* and some pieces in Muriel Leung's *Bone Confetti*. It may be a direct countermotion to the "nature-ness" of *Attendance*.

RMK: Definitely practices and experiences that left a mark in nature as a child, a teen, a twentysomething that are still with me. I could recount these for hours, seriously. Those are mostly from the Blue Ridge of the Appalachian Mountains, and from the high desert, the Mojave.

A reading where I heard an excerpt from a project from Melora Walters which, as far as I know, hasn't appeared yet but I hope will someday. Books and writers I first encountered on the syllabi of Jen Hofer for a course she renews over and over again called "Documentary Poetics." (Idk if the name has changed.)

Books and events that Los Ángeles-based poets and presses have given in the past year or so, including Writ Large Press's '90x90' and a series/practice called "Un.Fade.Able," which started and evolves as a response to the life and death of Sandra Bland; I hate being specific because there is a list of people and I'll always leave someone off because I get too distracted fangirling about someone else!! But people whose poetry might be really different from my own, that's been important. And experiencing poetry through my ears–very challenging for me, in a good way.

Also, for the first time in my life, I have spent a significant amount of time reading fanfic and thinking about fandom/participating as a fan in the past two or so years. I have NO idea where that is taking me as a writer, but it feels disingenuous not to include it. Particularly the work of a specific fanfic writer who I love and recently became the beta for. Like… what even is plot? I am fascinated by plot. Very related: I anticipate Ocean Vuong's novel with bated breath.

There's a really short answer to this question which is: going outside.

Does your process of naming (poems, sections, etc) influence you and/or color your work specifically? How did you approach the poems in this collection, together? Was the process of naming also a sort of collaborative Attendance? *Would you say, in a way, that poetics is always a sort of* Attendance? *or, always has the potential to be?*

RMK: Yes.

RC: As much as the tendency to name is why this work exists, there were so many times we didn't. People mostly. Even though it was election year, we didn't mention Trump once. We didn't always spell names of people in our month, or even famous people (Leonard Cohen, Prince, Bowie). And we didn't always name the Black men and Black women murdered by police. And yet, every Tuesday at Art Share during the Un.Fade.Able season we were literally there, saying Sandra Bland's name, saying all the names. Those days in November we were in the street. In late December during the community burial it is our practice to be with each other when we can and to read the names of the community dead. Because the poet is not only on the page.

RMK: Sooo much to say about this—the last time I wrote down an Ars Poetica it was paying attention—and before that it was taking responsibility for the meaning you make and before that naming—but at the same time, Attendance responds to this question for me, I'll leave off here.

Why is such a practice important to you? what does it represent as indicative of your method/ creative practice? your history? your mission/intentions/hopes/plans? What does, or might, this book do (as much as what it says or contains)? What would be the best possible outcome for this book? What might it do in the world, and how will its presence as an object facilitate your creative role in your community and beyond? What are your hopes for this book, and for your practice?

RC: The answer to this is an Ars Poetica. It is paying attention. Or making a map. It's my plan, my goal, the thing I do in my sleep and with all my wits about me.

Intentions are meaningless if the impact is the opposite, but my intention is to have made a map of the year and the place and the lives, to make the small things possible: here is how we lived in that year of drought, in that year our countrymen showed themselves to us. We shall see what the book does.

RMK: If it *does* something in the world, that is pretty damn cool already? Idk my highest ambition is probably that at least one person re-reads this book. Wait, okay ambition. That it changes (fucks with) the reader's perception as they move through the world. Sharpens them—ack! Feelings and sense-ings are the Worst!—and holds space for those feelings and sense-ings at the same time. (To be poetry that needs aftercare and is aftercare.)

Also if *Attendance* joined the family of almanacs; of praying the hours, of liturgy where there's a portion of holy text for each day, of reading to one another; cookbooks, spellbooks, commonplace books; book-objects that are read by flipping randomly to a page; to be scrolling through fandom and memes on tumblr and see *Attendance* quoted. Oh my fucking stars what if that happened?!?!?!

Do you plan to continue working together? What is next for each of you?

RC: Muahahaha we are shackled together for eternity.

RMK: Jaja totally. Working together will look the same and different. I haven't read Rocío's book (omFg I cannot wait for Spring 2019) but in some strange way I was still a companion to its writing. I think. Was I?

RC: Yes nerd.

Let's talk a little bit about the role of poetics and creative community in social activism, in particular in what I call "Civil Rights 2.0," which has remained immediately present all around us.

RC: I said before that my poetics cannot be separate from my desperation to survive. When I say survive I mean visibility and thriving-ness. Even writing is an insistence on these things. And as a Poet, which is to say a Person, I am in the world, not turning away. But because I am a Person, not a Robot, I also have periods of solitude to repair and prepare. The popular imagination has a white dude typing by candlelight, alone and shut away from the world and while also holding this sort of "outsider" or "rebel" status. EYEROLL EMOJI RIGHT HERE. Also, in my world, to be a poet is to take up space and make room to pull others through, which is the wirecutter idea.

RMK: Taking up space = acutely uncomfortable, particularly in this city, and that is as it should be. I'm a born-and-raised white-settler-culture woman. Whiteness feeds on attention but must be attended to. I don't know… I don't want my poet-life or my activist-life to be externally-processing whiteness at all times; it's just not the space I want to take up; it's not what I want to ask my community to constantly process with/for me.

At the same time I'm obsessed with where I come from, and there's no way to be from the Blue Ridge of the Appalachian Mountains without contending with whiteness and class and genocide and the survivors of genocide, particularly Cherokee people, and slavery and Afrolachia; and music and the natural world and geology and the list goes on and it's all in me so it's in the choices I make about justice and healing in the world.

Ummm I LOVE what Rocío wrote in response to this question. I want to say FUCK YES to the cosmic here-ness (lol) of every person and she is one of the people I pay attention to in order to see a way that might look. Poet = human = do the work = not just poetry. Um but it is cool when poetry can shove (or gently but firmly nudge) a reader/listener into a new place, for example, a place of: oh Fuck, I am a person who lives in a house and the person I walk by who is sleeping on the sidewalk of the street we share is my *neighbor* NOW WHAT.

I'd be curious to hear some thoughts on the challenges we face in speaking and publishing across lines of race, age, privilege, dis/ability, class, social/cultural background, and sexuality within the community, vs. the dangers of remaining and producing in isolated "silos."

RC: I literally don't understand. The best I can say is to, no matter how you "person" in the world as a speaker or publisher, center the voices of the marginalized.

RMK: Yes, this. And some folks I really respect have spoken about writing to and for their community. Bridgette Bianca and Never Ångeline Nørth aka Moss Angel come to mind. To be invited to also read, listen, sometimes publish, share, their work… that feels like the biggest most generous gift I could receive as a person.

Is there anything else you'd like to add?

RMK: Thank you for reading Attendance, Lynne!

RC: Thank you Lynne, for your important work and labor. We see you and appreciate you.

about the authors

ROCÍO CARLOS is the author of *(the other house)*, forthcoming from Civil Coping Mechanisms in 2019. She is also the author of *Coyolxhauqui, Los Angeles* (Archetype Press, 2012), *A World Below* (Mindmade Books, 2014), and co-author of *ex*her*pt* (wirecutter collective, 2016). She was selected as a 2003 Pen Center "Emerging Voices" fellow. She has infamous cats.

RACHEL MCLEOD KAMINER grew up in the Blue Ridge of the Appalachian Mountains. Her book of poetry *As in the dark, descend* was published with Writ Large Press in 2016. Rachel lives and works in Los Ángeles; she really likes to read.

The Operating System uses the language "print document" to differentiate from the book-object as part of our mission to distinguish the act of documentation-in-book-FORM from the act of publishing as a backwards-facing replication of the book's agentive *role* as it may have appeared the last several centuries of its history. Ultimately, I approach the book as TECHNOLOGY: one of a variety of printed documents (in this case, bound) that humans have invented and in turn used to archive and disseminate ideas, beliefs, stories, and other evidence of production.

Ownership and use of printing presses and access to (or restriction of printed materials) has long been a site of struggle, related in many ways to revolutionary activity and the fight for civil rights and free speech all over the world. While (in many countries) the contemporary quotidian landscape has indeed drastically shifted in its access to platforms for sharing information and in the widespread ability to "publish" digitally, even with extremely limited resources, the importance of publication on physical media has not diminished. In fact, this may be the most critical time in recent history for activist groups, artists, and others to insist upon learning, establishing, and encouraging personal and community documentation practices. Hear me out.

With The OS's print endeavors I wanted to open up a conversation about this: the ultimately radical, transgressive act of creating PRINT /DOCUMENTATION in the digital age. It's a question of the archive, and of history: who gets to tell the story, and what evidence of our life, our behaviors, our experiences are we leaving behind? We can know little to nothing about the future into which we're leaving an unprecedentedly digital document trail — but we can be assured that publications, government agencies, museums, schools, and other institutional powers that be will continue to leave BOTH a digital and print version of their production for the official record. Will we?

As a (rogue) anthropologist and long time academic, I can easily pull up many accounts about how lives, behaviors, experiences — how THE STORY of a time or place — was pieced together using the deep study of correspondence, notebooks, and other physical documents which are no longer the norm in many lives and practices. As we move our creative behaviors towards digital note taking, and even audio and video, what can we predict about future technology that is in any way assuring that our stories will be accurately told – or told at all? How will we leave these things for the record?

In these documents we say:
WE WERE HERE, WE EXISTED, WE HAVE A DIFFERENT STORY

- Elæ [Lynne DeSilva-Johnson], Founder/Creative Director
THE OPERATING SYSTEM, Brooklyn NY 2018

2019

Ark Hive-Marthe Reed
I Made for You a New Machine and All it Does is Hope - Richard Lucyshyn
Illusory Borders-Heidi Reszies
A Year of Misreading the Wildcats - Orchid Tierney
We Are Never The Victims - Timothy DuWhite
Of Color: Poets' Ways of Making | An Anthology of Essays on Transformative Poetics -
Amanda Galvan Huynh & Luisa A. Igloria, Editors

KIN(D)* Texts and Projects

A Bony Framework for the Tangible Universe-D. Allen
Opera on TV-James Brunton
Hall of Waters-Berry Grass
Transitional Object-Adrian Silbernagel

Glossarium: Unsilenced Texts and Translations

Śnienie / Dreaming - Marta Zelwan/Krystyna Sakowicz, (Poland, trans. Victoria Miluch)
Alparegho: Pareil-À-Rien / Alparegho, Like Nothing Else - Hélène Sanguinetti
(France, trans. Ann Cefola)
High Tide Of The Eyes - Bijan Elahi (Farsi-English/dual-language)
trans. Rebecca Ruth Gould and Kayvan Tahmasebian
 In the Drying Shed of Souls: Poetry from Cuba's Generation Zero
Katherine Hedeen and Víctor Rodríguez Núñez, translators/editors
Street Gloss - Brent Armendinger with translations for Alejandro Méndez, Mercedes
Roffé, Fabián Casas, Diana Bellessi, and Néstor Perlongher (Argentina)
Operation on a Malignant Body - Sergio Loo (Mexico, trans. Will Stockton)
Are There Copper Pipes in Heaven - Katrin Ottarsdóttir
(Faroe Islands, trans. Matthew Landrum)

2019 CHAPBOOKS

Print::Document Chapbook Series (7th Annual)

Vela. - Knar Gavin
[零] A Phantom Zero - Ryu Ando
RE: Verses - Kristina Darling and Chris Campanioni
Don't Be Scared - Magdalena Zurawski

Digital Chapbook Series (2018-19)

The American Policy Player's Guide and Dream Book - Rachel Zolf
Flight of the Mothman - Gyasi Hall
Mass Transitions - Sue Landers
The George Oppen Memorial BBQ - Eric Benick

2018

Glossarium: Unsilenced Texts and Translations

2018 CHAPBOOK SERIES (6TH ANNUAL)

for our full catalog please visit:
https://squareup.com/store/the-operating-system/

deeply discounted Book of the Month and Chapbook Series subscriptions
are a great way to support the OS's projects and publications!
sign up at: http://www.theoperatingsystem.org/subscribe-join/

DOC U MENT
/däkyəmənt/

First meant "instruction" or "evidence," whether written or not.

noun - a piece of written, printed, or electronic matter that provides information or evidence or that serves as an official record
verb - record (something) in written, photographic, or other form
synonyms - paper - deed - record - writing - act - instrument

[*Middle English, precept, from Old French, from Latin documentum, example, proof, from docre, to teach; see dek- in Indo-European roots.*]

Who is responsible for the manufacture of value?

Based on what supercilious ontology have we landed in a space
where we vie against other creative people in vain pursuit
of the fleeting credibilities of the scarcity economy, rather than
freely collaborating and sharing openly with each other
in ecstatic celebration of MAKING?

While we understand and acknowledge the economic pressures and fear-mongering that
threatens to dominate and crush the creative impulse, we also believe that
now more than ever we have the tools to relinquish agency via cooperative means,
fueled by the fires of the Open Source Movement.

Looking out across the invisible vistas of that rhizomatic parallel country
we can begin to see our community beyond constraints,
in the place where intention meets
resilient, proactive, collaborative organization.

Here is a document born of that belief, sown purely of imagination and will.
When we document we assert. We print to make real, to reify our being there.
When we do so with mindful intention to address our process,
to open our work to others, to create beauty in words in space,
to respect and acknowledge the strength of the page
we now hold physical, a thing in our hand,
we remind ourselves that, like Dorothy:
we had the power all along, my dears.

THE PRINT! DOCUMENT SERIES
is a project of
the trouble with bartleby
in collaboration with
the operating system

CPSIA information can be obtained
at www.ICGtesting.com
Printed in the USA
FSHW010606030620
70857FS

9 781946 031327